SADDAM SPEAKS ON THE GULF CRISIS

A COLLECTION OF DOCUMENTS

The Moshe Dayan Center for Middle Eastern and African Studies
The Shiloah Institute
Tel Aviv University

The Moshe Dayan Center, through the Shiloah Research Institute and its other constituent units, seeks to contribute by research, documentation, and publication to the study and understanding of the modern history and current affairs of the Middle East and Africa. The Center, with the Department of Middle Eastern and African History, is part of the School of History at Tel Aviv University. This study appears in the Center's Research and Teaching Aids Series.

Ṣaddam Speaks on the Gulf Crisis

A Collection of Documents

OFRA BENGIO

The Moshe Dayan Cetner for Middle Eastern and African Studies
The Shiloah Institute
Tel-Aviv University

OCLC 26372800

ISBN: 965-224-011-7

cover design: Ruth Beth-Or
typesetting and printing: 'Graph Chen' Press Ltd., Jerusalem

*To Shmuel
Lavi and Adi*

Contents

PREFACE

Iraq's occupation of Kuwait in August 1990 took the world by surprise. No less surprising were its positions and policies in the aftermath of the occupation, which led it into a head-on confrontation with friend and foe alike, trapped in a war of its own making. Iraq's behavior became even more enigmatic when Iraq revealed itself prepared to defy an unprecedented worldwide coalition of 28 nations, led by no less than the largest power in the world — the US — and supported by other Western as well as Arab and Muslim countries.

In order to better understand this unique chapter in the history of Iraq and the world at large, it would be helpful to follow the speeches of the main protagonist — President Saddam Husayn — during the year of crisis: February 1990-February 1991. Until such time as the archives of this period are opened, these speeches will remain an indispensable source for understanding Iraqi moves and motives. They are of particular importance in the study of a totalitarian regime such as that of the Iraqi Ba'th where the president had the first and last say on every matter, big and small, and where he became Iraq's sole spokesman to the world. Beyond providing a general outline of the development of the crisis, they also provide a rare insight into Saddam Husayn's personality, and even more important, into Iraq's political discourse, which became part and parcel of the conflict itself.

Roughly speaking, the period can be divided into three major phases. The first phase, from the beginning of 1990 until the occupation on 2 August, was characterized by Saddam Husayn's launching and developing what may be termed his grand strategy. What is peculiar about the speeches during this period is that they truly revealed Iraq's aggressive intentions, camouflaging only the exact target, which turned out to be Kuwait rather than Israel.

The second phase, from the occupation until the beginning of war on 17 January 1991, can be described as the period of digging in. Here again Saddam Husayn's speeches left no doubt as to Iraq's clear and unequivocal intention of keeping Kuwait for itself. In the last phase, the period of the war itself, Saddam Husayn had to go on the defensive, though he did not give up his defiant posture altogether. He had to come to terms with a terrible military defeat while attempting to sweeten it with talk of a great Iraqi victory.

There are a number of points particularly revealing in Saddam Husayn's speeches. For example, the extensive use of Koranic verses and Islamic phraseology, something which was quite rare at the beginning of his political career; the disproportionate emphasis on external issues at the expense of domestic ones; and the ambiguity and vagueness of some of his utterances. To a certain extent this last point could be attributed to problems of transmission and translation, but more often than not it was due to Husayn's own purposeful or unintentional vagueness.

In order to enable the reader to better navigate in the maze of speeches, an introductionary essay is included, based on my chapter on Iraq in the *Middle East Contemporary Survey* of the year 1990. The introduction provides a general framework for the crisis and an analysis of Iraq's motives and constraints. It does not however, discuss Iraqi domestic issues or other points not related to the crisis, for which the reader may consult the chapter on Iraq in that volume of the *Survey*.

This book was made possible through the encouragement and generous sharing of ideas on the part of my friends at the Moshe Dayan Center. I am especially grateful to Asher Susser, David Menashri, Ami Ayalon, and Bruce Maddy-Weitzman. Ety Faridian did a wonderful job as my right-hand in finding the sources; Lydia Gareh and Margaret Mahleb typed the manuscript with endless patience and care; and last but not least, Edna Liftman helped organize the whole enterprise.

Ofra Bengio

THE STRUGGLE FOR KUWAIT: VISION AND REALITY

SADDAM HUSAYN'S GRAND STRATEGY

Twice in one decade Iraq took the world by surprise: in September 1980 it invaded Iran and in August 1990 it invaded Kuwait. At first glance, these two incidents seem to be separate, but deeper analysis reveals that they are closely interrelated. In fact, the second invasion was meant to correct the stalemate caused by the first.

There are similarities between the two invasions that have had far-reaching implications. In both cases, Iraq's ruling Ba'th Party took a step no previous Iraqi regime had dared to take, despite the fact that both the border conflict with Iran and Iraq's claim to Kuwait went back to the beginning of the modern Iraqi state. In each case, Iraq went to war against a country that seemed much weaker, hoping for a quick victory. Iraqi rhetoric prior to both invasions focused on the Arab-Israeli conflict, but the subsequent military activity was directed at the Gulf region. In the event, both invasions turned into challenges to the regional and world economic order, and became traps for Baghdad.

The invasion of Kuwait underscored paradoxes which appeared to be unresolvable. How was it that a country which was expected to devote itself to reconstruction after a bloody war embarked instead on yet another military adventure? How was it that Iraq managed to mislead and surprise a world presumably familiar with Iraqi rhetoric and methods? And how did a country which emerged from the Gulf War undefeated due primarily to aid from the Gulf states and the West, begin to challenge the West before first settling its conflict with Iran?

It appears that the key to understanding these paradoxes lies in the stalemate that marked the end of the Gulf War, which put Iraq under tremendous pressure to reach an agreement with Iran. Although Iraq portrayed the stalemate as a major victory, the war did not achieve Baghdad's minimal aim of ensuring Iraqi sovereignty over the Shatt al-'Arab waterway, which Iraq gave up in the 1975 Algiers agreement. Without achieving this goal, Iraq remained virtually landlocked, dependent on neighboring states for shipping, and the eight-year war was rendered meaningless.

Alongside these pressures, Iraq had to face the realities of a changing world order: the crumbling of the Soviet bloc, the emergence of the United States as the sole world power and the wave of democratization which swept Eastern Europe and threatened to spill over into the Middle East. The combination of these internal, regional and international pressures, together with long-held ambitions of turning Iraq into a regional, and Third World power, drove President Saddam Husayn to develop what one might call "Husayn's grand strategy," which became the prologue to the invasion of Kuwait.

The four-point strategy, which he began developing at the start of the year, was designed to: (1) contain internal economic, social, and political pressures by diverting attention to external issues; (2) unite the Arab and Islamic world around Iraq, as well as reduce Iranian hostility to it, by launching an anti-Israel and anti-American campaign with distinct Islamic overtones; (3) lead to a peaceful solution to the conflict with Iran through direct contacts starting in April 1990, and hints of a major Iraqi concession on the Shatt al-'Arab; and (4) prepare the ground for the occupation of Kuwait by carrying on the oil dispute with it *ad absurdum*. Emphasizing the oil aspect of the dispute was another Iraqi diversionary tactic meant to mislead Kuwait and the world into believing that oil prices and not territorial ambitions were at stake.

The primary object of the invasion was to compensate Iraq for giving up the Shatt al-'Arab and ensure an outlet to the sea, which would solve Iraq's geostrategic problems. The invasion also held the promise of other benefits for Iraq: vast sources of oil and money, and the consolidation of Iraqi claims to leadership of the Gulf region and the entire Arab world. Baghdad, to be sure, emphasized the ideological reason for the invasion — the need for Arab unity — along with the historical cause of correcting the wrongs of British imperialism, which was blamed for tearing away Kuwait from Iraq. Certain lessons of the war with Iran influenced Iraq's decision to invade Kuwait. Despite vital Western interests in the Gulf, no one had come to Iran's rescue. In fact, by the end of the war, most countries were on Iraq's side despite the fact that Baghdad was the aggressor. Iraq was further reinforced by the knowledge that the world had done nothing when Iraq used chemical weapons against Kurdish civilians in 1988. The Iraqi regime had also learned that it could manipulate countries into assisting it in its military buildup and ignoring its development and use of nonconventional weapons.

To Iraq's surprise, however, this time the world did not react as it had previously. The invasion of Kuwait appeared so outrageous, that it united friends and foes against Iraq. If before the invasion Iraq dictated the rules of the international game which it had initiated, afterward, it was forced to maneuver and improvise according to the rules of others. Furthermore, as easy as the occupation turned out to be, it became extremely difficult for Iraq to hold on to Kuwait. Thus the war on Kuwait, which was meant to rectify the results of an earlier war, only led to a third one in January 1991, but with more catastrophic results for the Iraqi state and people.

CHALLENGING THE UNITED STATES

Seen in retrospect, Iraq renewed a policy of confrontation with the US from the beginning of 1990. For almost two decades, during 1967–84, the two countries had not maintained diplomatic relations because Iraq opposed Washington's "imperialist" policy and "pro-Israeli bias." But when relations were resumed during the war with Iran, due mainly to the pressures of war, Baghdad toned down its propaganda in order to gain American diplomatic, political, economic, and technological support. The return to the previous line at the beginning of 1990 was an Iraqi initiative, part of Iraq's grand strategy in various areas. The shift, however, was misinterpreted in Washington, and an asymmetry in their relations developed during the first half of 1990: the stronger the Iraqi attacks on the US, the greater the American tendency to appease Iraq.

Officially, Iraq related the change in its policy to US anti-Iraqi and anti-Arab positions on various issues, chief of which was what Baghdad described as active support for the immigration of Soviet Jews to Israel as well as US recognition of united Jerusalem as the capital of Israel. Iraq accused the US of using "the Zionist entity as a tool to safeguard its interest in the region."[1] Another issue of great concern to Baghdad was the criticism in the American press of Iraq's human rights record, which peaked following the execution of British journalist Farzad Bazoft on 15 March. An issue of even greater concern was US cooperation with Great Britain in unearthing the secret Iraqi network for the procurement of nuclear and other nonconventional weapons. The disclosures threatened to jeopardize the development of Iraq's nuclear and other nonconventional weapons, which was the most ambitious part of Iraq's strategy.

The regime had turned the army in general and the military industry in particular into the most important political prop for advancing its ambitions at home and in the region, and the disclosures therefore, were a significant setback. Baghdad used all these issues to develop the theme of a triangular Zionist-American-British anti-Iraqi conspiracy. However, antagonizing as these issues might have been, they were only pretexts for the new Iraqi policy. The development that truly motivated Iraq to reappraise its policies was the collapse of the Communist bloc in Eastern Europe and the emergence of the US as the world's sole superpower. Rather than inducing Iraq to strengthen its ties with the US, the change in Eastern Europe encouraged Baghdad to challenge Washington.

Baghdad's new strategy was the outcome of a number of conflicting forces: its self-perception, severe domestic problems,

---

1. Iraqi News Agency, 28 June — DR, 29 June 1990.

and longtime aspirations. The rapid development of its military machine gradually led Iraq to conceive of itself as capable of leading not only the Arab world but also the entire Third World in challenging the US and obstructing its designs for a "new world order." This policy had a particular relevance in the Persian Gulf area, where Iraq harbored long-standing hegemonic aspirations that had been thwarted by the US-Iranian alliance in the 1970s and by the war with Iran in the 1980s. The emergence of Iraq as the victor in the war, the weakening of Iran in the aftermath of the war, and the vacuum created by the changes in Eastern Europe convinced Baghdad to make its bid for leadership in the Gulf by removing the last obstacle, namely, the US presence there. Standing up to the US was also designed to lay the groundwork for a *rapprochement* with Iran. Mindful of Iran's deep ideological and political enmity toward the US, Iraq sought to exploit its newfound enmity toward the US to enhance its ideological affinity, as it were, with Iran.

Saddam Husayn set the stage for the new approach to the US in his 24 February 1990 speech at the meeting of the Arab Cooperation Council, the alliance of Iraq, Egypt, Jordan, and North Yemen. Speaking on behalf of all Arabs, the president analyzed the new situation, focusing on the status of the US as the sole superpower, to the detriment of the Arabs. The power of the Soviet Union, which had been "the key champion of the Arabs in the context of the Arab-Israeli conflict," was eroded. The US, "with its known capitalist approach and its imperialist policies," could now penetrate the Arab world further and commit "follies against the interests and national security of the Arabs," while building up "an aggressive Israel" to serve its needs in the region. Saddam Husayn urged the Arab world to defy this new reality, not submit to it, because "there is no place among the ranks of good Arabs for the fainthearted who would argue that as a superpower, the US will be the decisive factor, and others have no choice but to submit."

To achieve this goal, Husayn suggested that the Arabs first and foremost should unite their forces and strengthen solidarity among themselves. He pointed out in this speech and elsewhere that such a policy was now more feasible than formerly because the erosion of communism had removed an important ideological and political barrier separating the various Arab regimes. At the same time, the Arabs should clarify to the US that the Arab nation was "a great nation that taught humanity things it had been ignorant of," and that it was capable of using weapons against the US and the West. Husayn alluded to the possibility of once again using the oil weapon, which had been "so effective" during the war in October 1973. Another way of putting pressure on the US was to divert "hundreds of billions" of dollars invested by the Arabs in the US and the West to the USSR and East European countries. Most important of all, however, was to call on the US to withdraw its fleet from the Persian Gulf, where its presence might have been necessary during the Iraqi-Iranian War, but where it had become a menace, because the US presence "in the most important spot in the region and perhaps in the whole world" only increased its already immense power to influence the marketing and pricing of oil.[2]

SADDAM HUSAYN'S "NEW ARAB ORDER"

The changing world order was seen by Saddam Husayn as a historical opportunity for building a "new Arab order" which Iraq would lead. The claim to this role, which was long-standing, was given various old and new justifications. Saddam Husayn kept reiterating that Iraq had once been the center of Arab and world civilization, implying that now it was entitled to such a role once again. No less important was Iraq's recent role in confronting Iran in an eight-year war which not only saved the Arab nation from a catastrophe but also achieved the first Arab victory in hundreds of years. Furthermore, he maintained, Iraq's technological development, especially in the realm of weapons and military equipment, put it on a par with the West. In a speech on 2 April 1990, Saddam Husayn claimed that Iraq possessed the binary chemical weapon which only two superpowers possessed, an achievement, he claimed,

2.   Amman TV, 24 February — DR, 27 February 1990.

which gave the Arabs strategic balance with Israel even though the Arabs did not possess nuclear weapons. Above all, Iraq was headed by "a unique leader," namely Saddam Husayn. For years, the Iraqi media and various books published about Saddam Husayn had developed his image as a leader of historical stature, to be compared only with the greatest of leaders in Arab and Islamic history from Muhammad to Salah al-Din al-Ayyubi.[3]

Although the configuration of this "new Arab order" was not fully revealed at the beginning of the year, elements of it emerged clearly: the Arabs can and should play an influential role in the world, and even impose their will on it, because of the political and economic power, namely oil that they possess; this influence could be enhanced by confrontation with the "imperialist" powers, chiefly the US and Britain, rather than by coming to terms with them; and force, not peaceful means, would solve the Palestine question. Baghdad had to convince the Arab world of the validity and feasibility of this vision. It had to contend with Arab regimes which feared growing Iraqi might, such as the Gulf states, or opposed Iraq's political line, such as Egypt, or were outright enemies, such as Syria.

At the beginning of the year, Iraq organized a wide-ranging propaganda campaign aimed at allaying the fears of Arab governments and arousing the enthusiasm of the Arab masses for the Iraqi vision. In what turned out to be the most cynical of Iraq's efforts to reassure its fellow Arabs, Husayn repeatedly called for basing inter-Arab relations on the principles of "noninterference in internal affairs' and "nonuse of force" among Arabs.[4] At the same time, however, Iraq resorted to an unprecedented level of demagoguery concerning the "smear" campaign against Iraq by Israel and the West, which it labeled "ferocious." What was peculiar

3. For two such books see Sabah Salman, *Saddam Husayn Qa'id Wa-ta'rikh* (Baghdad: sharikat matba'at al-adib, 1986); Zuhayr Sadiq Rida al-Khalidi, *Al-Qiyam 'Inda Saddam Husayn* (Baghdad: dar al-hurriya lil-tiba'a, 1989).
4. E.g., Iraqi News Agency, 18 January, 22 February — DR, 19 January, 23 February 1990.

to this Iraqi policy was that Iraq posed both as the hero and the victim. It manipulated the Bazoft affair, as well as Husayn's threat to incinerate half of Israel, in order to raise a hue and cry regarding Zionist and Western conspiracies against Iraq and to organize all-Arab support for Iraq. The Iraqis argued that the Zionist-Western conspiracies were directed not only against Iraq but against "the Arab nation, its existence and its national security."[5] However, Iraq was capable not only of thwarting these conspiracies, but also of achieving for the Arabs "power and loftiness," for which millions of Arabs had been yearning. The slogan that kept appearing was "united we stand, divided we fall."[6]

This slogan, however, could not disguise the polarization in the Arab world which emerged at the emergency summit held in Baghdad at the end of May 1990. Convened at Iraqi insistence, the summit was officially scheduled to deal with the Palestinian question and the immigration of Soviet Jews to Israel, but, in fact, it was intended to mobilize Arab support for Baghdad and its leadership role. The summit, held 12 years after the last summit in the Iraqi capital in 1978, came full circle: in 1978, Baghdad led the Arab world in ostracizing Egypt for its peace negotiations with Israel; in 1990, it again took the lead in rejecting any peaceful solution for the dispute with Israel, denying Israel's very existence, and calling for the liberation of Palestine by force.

ATTITUDES TOWARD ISRAEL: IRAQ'S DOUBLE ROLE
OF WOLF AND LAMB

After a decade of relative aloofness from the Arab-Israeli conflict, Iraq made it the focus of its rhetoric, a change that was both quantitative and qualitative. President Husayn himself led the campaign, which surpassed all previous Ba'th campaigns in its intensity and militancy. There was a return to slogans that had long been subdued, such as liberating Palestine and destroying Israel,

---

5. Iraqi News Agency, 12 April — DR, 12 April 1990.
6. Iraqi News Agency, 18 April — DR, 19 April 1990.

and renewed talk of linkage between the three tiers of the conflict, namely, the Palestinian question, Iraq's conflict with Israel, and the Arab-Israeli conflict in general.

In his Army Day speech on 5 January 1990, President Husayn warned Israel against attacking Iraq's scientific and military installations, promising that Iraq would react.[7] He returned to the issue in two speeches in February, the first speech reiterating a warning against possible "Israeli military aggression" which might lead to "the occupation of new lands,"[8] the second introducing a new-old offensive note — the "liberation of Palestine." Declaring that Palestine had been usurped as a result of deliberate planning and, therefore, could only be regained by such means, Husayn expressed his conviction that "Palestine will return" and that "the banners of justice shall fly over holy Jerusalem."[9] At the end of March he again made a speech dedicated entirely to the issue of liberating Palestine. Claiming to speak on behalf of all Arabs, he argued that the Arabs were of one mind "for liberated Palestine" and were capable of achieving it if they showed determination and faith in God. Of all the Arabs, he said, the Iraqis were the most prepared to continue making sacrifices for the cause. They would not tire of wars, and Palestine was never far from Baghdad since it remained alive in the Iraqi conscience.[10]

What most captured world attention was Husayn's warning shortly afterward that "we will make fire eat up half of Israel if it tries to do anything against Iraq."[11] However, the strong international reaction to this declaration did not lead Husayn to retract it. He explained that it was a defensive argument meant to deter Israel from attacking Iraq, and the attack he anticipated was an atomic one. He predicted that Soviet Jewish immigration to

7. *Al-Jumhuriyya* (Baghdad), 6 January 1990.
8. *Al-Thawra* (Baghdad), 19 February 1990.
9. Ibid., 25 February 1990.
10. Ibid., 30 March 1990.
11. Ibid., 3 April 1990.

Israel would contribute to Israeli expansionism, akin to Hitler's *Lebensraum,* and that Iraq would not be dissuaded from demanding the rights usurped in Palestine. Moreover, he asserted, Iraq was doing the whole Islamic nation a service, for Palestine belonged to all Muslims. In April, adding a religious note to his position, he alluded to the notion of a Jihad against Israel.[12] Again, in June, he declared that the war against Israel was "inevitable" if Israel continued to seek to deport the Palestinians.[13]

Iraq's policy was attributed to fear of an Israeli attack against Iraqi installations similar to the one on the nuclear reactor in 1981. While this fear cannot be underestimated, it seems that the Israeli "danger" was exaggerated and that the Israeli card was skillfully played to serve various domestic and external purposes not necessarily connected with the issue of Israel. The Iraqi policy seems to have been well considered; Husayn himself said that the declaration on destroying half of Israel was neither impulsive nor emotional and that it had been decided upon by the state's leadership.[14] Domestically, the "imminent Israeli danger" was designed to rally dwindling support for the regime, justify the difficult economic and social conditions and explain why more than a year and a half after the end of the war with Iran, about 1 million soldiers were still mobilized, with no end to this situation in sight. Iraq sought to project the message that it was nearing strategic parity with Israel, and that although it did not yet possess nuclear weapons, the binary chemical weapon in its possession would create a balance of terror that would deter Israel from attacking Iraqi installations.

Externally, airing the slogan of the liberation of Palestine was designed to arouse dormant desires among the Arab masses and to rally them around Iraq. Iraq's policy was intended as an alternative

12. R. Baghdad, 16, 19 April, 28 May, 18, 30 June — DR, 17, 20 April, 29 May, 2 July 1990.
13. *Le Monde,* 30 June 1990.
14. *Al-Muharrir* (Paris), 8 May — DR, 9 May 1990.

to that advocated by Egypt and, above all, as a claim for Arab leadership. Iraq also utilized the threats against Israel as a warning to its Arab partners and as a diversion, which was proved by the occupation of Kuwait. Moreover, the attacks on Israel served as a warning to the West, especially to Britain and the US, which were now mentioned in the same breath with Israel, not to attempt to block Iraq's development of nonconventional weapons. Above all, however, Iraq's message was aimed at Iran.

THE CHANGE OF HEART TOWARD IRAN

With the Iraq-Iran cease-fire in August 1988, Iraq's main concern was to achieve a peaceful agreement with Iran. However, repeated attempts by Baghdad to break the deadlock by initiating talks with Iran were unsuccessful: Five rounds of indirect talks held under UN auspices ended in naught. Accordingly, by the beginning of 1990, Baghdad had come to the conclusion that progress would depend on concessions to Iran, and would necessitate a change in orientation. In a move reminiscent of the volte-face of 1975 toward Iran, Iraq attempted to restore confidence between the two countries. But whereas in 1975 the Iraqi change had been Western-oriented in order to win the pro-Western Shah's goodwill, in 1990 the change was anti-Western and pro-Islamic in order to gain the support of the Islamic fundamentalist regime in Tehran.

The most important ideological concession to Iran was the adoption by the secular Ba'thi regime of the mantle of Islam, emphasizing Islamic values, symbols, and slogans. In contrast with the past decade, when the Islamic revolution and "religious fanaticism" in Iran had been vilified as the main enemy of Iraq and the Arab world as a whole, Saddam Husayn now sought to turn Islam into a bridge for *rapprochement* and a vehicle for forging a common Arab-Islamic front against Israel. "We have nothing to fear from waging our struggle under the precepts of Islam and its benevolent principles," he declared. Husayn emphasized that there was no contradiction whatsoever between carrying on the struggle under the banner of Islam anywhere in the world, and Arabism, because the "true struggle makes Arabism and Islam one thing rather than two separate things."[15]

Along with this ideological shift, Iraq also made political overtures to Iran, to which the latter reacted positively. Thus, on 27 July, the first talks were held in Geneva at the foreign minister level with the participation of UN Secretary-General Javier Pérez de Cuellar. By that time, the ideological and political *rapprochement* had acquired an economic dimension. As in the 1975 Algiers agreement, oil again played an important part in bringing the two countries closer. In the July controversy over oil policies between Iraq, on the one hand, and Kuwait and the United Arab Emirates, on the other, Iran sided unequivocally with Iraq. Commenting on the border disputes between Iraq and Kuwait, Iran displayed understanding of Iraq's claims when it said that Iraq needed the two islands of Warba and Bubiyan "as [an] entry point to the Persian Gulf."[16]

THE EXECUTION OF A STRATEGY

"THE RETURN OF KUWAIT TO THE MOTHERLAND"

During the 70 years of its modern history, Iraq has made three major attempts, under three different regimes, to annex Kuwait. All three attempts reflected not only the expansionist ambitions of the men at the country's helm, but also deep-rooted popular historical and geopolitical grievances, namely, that during Ottoman rule Kuwait had been part of the Vilayet of Basra, but the British, by "carving" Kuwait out of Iraq, had left Iraq with such a short coastline that the country was left at the mercy of its neighbors and hence under virtual siege.[17]

---

15. Iraqi News Agency, 26 June — DR, 27 June 1990.
16. R. Tehran, 19 July — DR, 19 July 1990. A later report claimed that Saddam Husayn informed Rafsanjani about the coming invasion and even suggested a "strategic alliance" with Iran. *International Herald Tribune,* 21 March 1991.
17. For a discussion of the historical relationship between Iraq and Kuwait, see

It is not clear when the military preparations for the occupation of Kuwait began. Some claim that they were begun three to five years previously, others only a few months prior to August 1990. Possibly the idea was considered a few years earlier in reaction to Iran's occupation of Faw in February 1986, but it certainly received impetus as a result of the stalemate in the peace talks with Iran. The plainest indication of Iraqi plans appeared in an article in early March 1990 in *Sourakia,* which seemed to have been leaked by Iraqi sources. The strongly anti-Kuwaiti article made these points:

(1) The return of Kuwait to "the motherland," Iraq, had preoccupied every Iraqi ruler from Nuri al-Saʻid to Saddam Husayn.

(2) The Iranian occupation of Faw in 1986 highlighted Iraq's severe strategic maritime problem, which could be solved only by Kuwait. However, Kuwait was reluctant to cooperate. It refused to lease the island of Bubiyan to Iraq and thereby give it access to the open sea.

(3) The Iraqi demand of the American naval forces in February 1990 to leave the Gulf implied that a foreign power was blocking the Iraqi claim for "the return of Kuwait to the motherland."

(4) The problems between Iraq and Kuwait were not merely border problems, but questions of "fate" and "existence." At this point, "the fate of Kuwait has become open to discussion."[18]

In building up the "Kuwaiti crisis," Iraq resorted to tactics it had used in developing previous artificial crises with the West and Israel, namely diversionary strategies, ambiguous messages, victimization, and the escalation of threats, which in this case culminated in the use of force. By far the most important of these devices was that described in the Arabic adage: "He beat me but he cried out, he got the start on me but he complained." The complaint focused on the issue of oil, rather than territory, first because Iraq made seemingly

Uriel Dann, *The Iraqi Invasion of Kuwait: Historical Observations,* The Moshe Dayan Center, Data and Analysis, August 1990. See also, Husain M. al-Bahara, *The Legal Status of the Arabian Gulf States* (Manchester: Manchester University, 1968), pp. 250–58, chapter on Iraqi claim to sovereignty over Kuwait.

18.   *Sourakia* (London), 5 March 1990.

justified claims regarding oil, and second because it could turn oil into a cause that would rally diverse countries around it, including Iran, other Arab oil-producing countries, and poorer states.

Saddam Husayn chose to bring the crisis out into the open in his 17 July 1990 anniversary speech. Attacking the new oil policy of several of the Gulf states, he claimed that it had resulted in an annual loss of $1 billion in Iraq's revenues. Husayn accused these states of acting upon the inspiration of the US and of aiming to strike at "pan-Arab security and interests" by thrusting their "poisoned dagger" into Iraq's back. Iraq, therefore, had "no choice but to resort to effective action to put things right."[19]

Meanwhile, Iraq publicly aired the border problem between the two countries. On 24 July it published the contents of a letter sent to Kuwait on 30 April to the effect that the border issue had "at no time been [simply] a technical issue" and that what Kuwait called an agreement on the issue — presumably the 1963 agreement[20] — had "neither *de jure* nor *de facto* effect...it is long over and done with."[21] On 24 July Iraq began massing 30,000 troops along its border with Kuwait while the Iraqi media spoke of "Iraq's legitimate rights" in Kuwait.

Iraq's purposely ambiguous stance and its initial stress on oil policy deluded the world into believing that oil prices and quotas were the chief issue in its dispute with Kuwait, and that if this issue were solved, things might return to normal. Iraq carefully prepared a deceptive plan and an alibi. At the Arab summit in May, Saddam Husayn harshly attacked unnamed oil-producing countries for waging economic war, which was tantamount to a military move against Iraq. Since the attack was made at a closed meeting, the Arab leaders in attendance sought to keep the issue within the Arab

19.   R. Baghdad, 17 July — DR, 17 July 1990.
20.   On 4 October 1963, the first Ba'thi regime (February-November 1963) headed by the then Prime Minister Ahmad Hasan al-Bakr, recognized "the independence and full sovereignty of Kuwait." R. Baghdad, 4 October — DR, 7 October 1963.
21.   *Al-Jumhuriyya* (Baghdad), 25 July 1990.

"family." But when Husayn made the issue public in his speech of 17 July, the reaction became much more agitated and outspoken. Iraq prepared an "alibi" *vis-à-vis* the US as well. Not only had it attacked the US for half a year, demanding that it leave the Gulf — a bad omen in itself — but, in an exceptional gesture, Saddam Husayn summoned April Glaspie, the US ambassador, to discuss the situation with her a week before the invasion. The aim of the meeting, as far as could be learned from a later Iraqi interpretation, was to give advance notice of Iraqi intentions and to assess the American reaction. Maintaining his aggressive tone against the US, Saddam Husayn vehemently attacked Kuwait and the United Arab Emirates for waging economic war against Iraq and warned that Baghdad's patience was running out. Glaspie, who went out of her way to reassure the president, seemed to have unintentionally given him encouragement for his future move when she reportedly said: "We have no opinion on the Arab-Arab conflicts, like your border disagreement with Kuwait."[22]

The war with Kuwait took place on 2 August 1990. The campaign was easy, speedy, and successful. Within seven hours, Iraq's 100,000 soldiers, most of them belonging to the elite Republican Guard force, overran Kuwait and subdued its much smaller, inexperienced army of c. 20,000 men. But, easy as the victory was, it became an increasingly difficult burden. Kuwait turned out to be a terrible political, military, and economic trap for Iraq. The surprise attack shocked not only Kuwait but the majority of Arab countries and the world at large. It constituted a breach of well- established Arab norms, violating a taboo on occupying another sovereign Arab state, an act which had never been perpetrated before.

Culminating months of ongoing threats and defiance on the part of Iraq, the invasion triggered a unified worldwide response hardly ever witnessed in the past. The reaction was as powerful as the shock, with Iraq as surprised at the world's reaction as the world at the Iraqi act. Iraq found itself contending with a daunting threefold

---

22. *New York Times,* 23 September 1990.

task of maintaining control over Kuwait, standing up to an ever-growing international coalition arrayed against it, and dealing with severe economic, social, and political consequences at home.

Iraqi policy in Kuwait aimed at achieving a single goal after the conquest: the quick Iraqization of Kuwait. On 8 August, Iraq formally announced the "merger" (*indimaj*) with Kuwait. The propaganda line depicting the invasion as a response to the Kuwaiti people's call was dropped altogether and was replaced by the claim that Iraq had historical rights to Kuwait. Blaming Western colonialism for having partitioned the Arab homeland into various states in order to weaken it, a Revolutionary Command Council statement singled out the Iraqi-Kuwaiti case for special emphasis. "Colonialism divested it [Iraq] of a dear part of it, namely Kuwait, and kept Iraq from the waters to prevent it from acquiring part of its tactical and strategic abilities and thus kept part of its people and part of its wealth away from the origin and the well spring." Expressing its contempt for Kuwait, which was "weak", "small," and lacking "cultural depth," the Revolutionary Command Council was determined "to rectify what time had wronged and to cancel the injustice and unfairness that had befallen Iraq." Accordingly, it decided "to return the segment and branch, Kuwait, to the whole and root, Iraq, in a comprehensive, eternal, and inseparable merger (*wahda indimajiyya*)."[23]

FACING THE WORLD

No sooner had Iraq occupied Kuwait than it faced a most difficult dilemma: holding on to Kuwait meant running the risk of political, economic, and military action against it by many Arab and non-Arab states, chief among them the US, while relinquishing Kuwait meant losing all the political, economic, and geostrategic gains it had hoped to achieve. Apparently, at a very early stage Iraq decided on the former option.

---

23. R. Baghdad, 8 August — DR, 9 August 1990.

As a result Iraq had to face political isolation, unprecedented economic sanctions, and the growing possibility of a war against it. But rather than convince Iraq to relinquish its position, these challenges only increased its determination to maintain it. A pattern of action and reaction emerged whereby additional pressure brought on Baghdad triggered immediate defiance and resolve to buttress the "unification" with Kuwait. These acts of defiance were a continuation of the policy adopted at the beginning of the year, only now it was implemented *ad absurdum*. From the occupation of Kuwait to the outbreak of war on 17 January 1991, Saddam Husayn and other officials never wavered in their decision to annex Kuwait. This was the unequivocal message to foreigners and to Iraqis alike.

Iraq's behavior resulted from the encounter of its vision of grandeur with the reality of severe economic, political, and military difficulties. Husayn's personality, particularly his ambition to go down in history as an Arab hero who had challenged the entire world, also played an important role. Additional factors that were responsible for Iraq's behavior were the constraints of the unresolved problem with Iran, which had first pushed Iraq to occupy Kuwait; the strong, if whimsical, belief that war was avoidable; and the feeling that should war erupt, Iraq could win it.

The firm international reaction to the occupation called for an immediate Iraqi attempt to break the anti-Iraqi coalition. Baghdad acted through a combination of threats, blackmail, promises, and pressures. On 12 August, Saddam Husayn launched a new initiative designed to free Iraq from its international isolation and to divert world attention to other issues — a "linkage" plan which contained three points:

(1) "The immediate and unconditional withdrawal of Israel from the occupied Arab territories in Palestine, Syria, and Lebanon"; the withdrawal of Syria from Lebanon; "a withdrawal between Iraq and Iran" (*sic*); and the "formulation of arrangements for the situation in Kuwait...taking into consideration the historical rights of Iraq in its territory and the Kuwaiti people's choice." Husayn stressed that the implementation of the plan should start with the oldest occupation of all, that by Israel.

(2) The immediate withdrawal of American and other forces from Saudi Arabia.

(3) An immediate freeze on all decisions to boycott Iraq and impose a state of siege on it.[24]

The coalition, perceiving the plan as another maneuver to keep Kuwait under Iraqi control, rejected it outright.

In another attempt to split the coalition and break the economic embargo, Husayn announced a promise of free Iraqi oil to all Third World countries, on 10 September, if they found a way to transport it. Explaining the motives behind this generosity, Husayn stressed that it was meant to "ease the burden" on Third World countries and "maintain solidarity with them."[25] However, this initiative failed as well.

IRAQ VERSUS THE WORLD'S STRONGEST POWER

From the outset, Iraq portrayed the Gulf crisis as essentially a conflict between two nations, two wills, and two leaders. As one Iraqi paper put it, "the crisis, though seemingly international and with worldwide implications" was between Iraq and the US.[26] In contrast to the first part of the year, when Iraq's challenge to the US was met with appeasement, after the occupation of Kuwait the US made a 180 degree change in policy. Iraq's earlier warnings about the US role in the area became a kind of self-fulfilling prophecy. The US led the global political alliance to isolate Iraq politically, economically, and militarily in order to force it to withdraw from Kuwait. It reacted promptly on 7 August by sending US troops to protect Saudi Arabia against a possible Iraqi attack; it prepared to take military action should sanctions fail to convince Iraq to withdraw, and it challenged the very legitimacy of Husayn's rule over Iraq. By comparing Saddam Husayn to Hitler, President George Bush made an implicit call for his ouster from power. Such a

---

24.   R. Baghdad, 12 August — DR, 13 August 1990.
25.   Baghdad TV, 10 September — DR, 12 September 1990.
26.   *Al-'Iraq* (Baghdad), 18 November — DR, 21 November 1990.

challenge, which was reminiscent of Ayatollah Ruhollah Khomeyni's challenge to Husayn during the Iraqi-Iranian War, only strengthened Husayn's resolve to stay in power and to stand up to Bush as he had done to Khomeyni. From the outset, Husayn portrayed himself as an equal to Bush, with the clash between them a conflict between two equal nations. Husayn believed in Iraq's ability to challenge the US, the sole world power, by attempting to unite the Arab world, the Islamic world, and the Third World around Iraq.

Attempting to counter the US-led economic and political steps against it, and to forestall a war against it, Iraq came to believe its own propaganda. The main themes of this propaganda were that the US, which had intervened by force in Grenada and Panama, could not dictate to Iraq to act differently; that the US deployment of forces in Saudi Arabia was another facet of its imperialist policy to safeguard its interests in the area, not to liberate Kuwait or defend Saudi Arabia as it claimed; that after the Vietnamese fiasco the US would not dare embark on an adventure in Kuwait; and that if war did break out, the US would certainly be the loser. Iraqi officials constantly belittled US air superiority, claiming that wars had never been decided by an air force.[27] They also stressed the different attitude toward death in the two societies: "Yours [the US] is a society which cannot accept 10,000 dead in one battle,"[28] while for Iraq, "death is an honor, we would be martyrs."[29] The language of threats became an integral part of Iraq's political discourse, directed especially against the US. For example, in an open letter to Bush on 16 August, Saddam Husayn predicted that "ten thousands of Americans wrapped up in sad coffins will reach you after you have sent them into a dark tunnel."[30] The Iraqi information minister warned foreign and American pilots that "they might be eaten up by

27. E.g., Saddam Husayn, Iraqi News Agency, 5 September — DR, 6 September 1990.
28. *New York Times*, 23 September 1990.
29. Iraqi News Agency, 20 August — DR, 21 August 1990.
30. R. Baghdad, 16 August — DR, 17 August 1990.

the people when their aircraft are downed. None of them will remain alive."[31]

By the end of the year Iraq declared to the world its willingness to fight back in what would become the "mother of battles" (*umm al-ma'arik*). Saddam Husayn appeared to be seeking an encounter with the world's strongest country and its allies, deluded by a vision of grandeur, invincibility and honor. The identification of the entire state with Saddam Husayn, and the lack of any significant political opposition, made the encounter a certainty.

ARABISM AND ISLAM: IRAQ'S STRATEGIC DEPTH

Iraq's feeling of encirclement was intensified by the policy of the Arab world on the crisis. Overall, the occupation shocked many Arab governments. Not only had it violated Arab rules and taboos, but Iraq's deployment of troops along the Saudi border after the invasion raised the specter of further Iraqi aggression in the region. The Arab League's immediate condemnation of the "Iraqi aggression" and its call for unconditional withdrawal was soon followed by a more substantial reaction when, on 10 August, at the emergency Arab summit in Cairo, a majority of 12 states out of 21 voted to send forces to the Gulf in order to check Iraq. What incensed Baghdad most was that three Arab states — Egypt, Syria, and Saudi Arabia — joined the US-led anti-Iraqi coalition and sent troops to support the demand for withdrawal. Iraq was particularly wary of Saudi Arabia, which had invited the US forces onto Saudi soil, and of Egypt, its erstwhile ally in the Arab Cooperation Council, which was considered the moving spirit behind the Arab anti-Iraqi coalition.

Faced with this coalition, Iraq tried to devise one of its own by transcending governments and appealing to the Arab and Muslim masses everywhere. Iraq hoped to use the masses to destabilize regimes or pressure them to change their policy in support of Iraq.

---

31. Iraqi News Agency, 20 August — DR, 21 August 1990.

In the encounter between a substantive coalition and a more abstract one, Iraq was counting on time to work in its favor. It built its strategy on three main bases: moving from the defensive to the offensive, diverting attention from Kuwait and appealing to deep Arab and Muslim sentiments and loyalties. The attack on the rich and corrupt Al Sabah family was justified by an old-new argument: the need for a just distribution of Arab wealth. Capitalizing on the tensions between rich and poor countries and the feelings of deprivation among great numbers of the Arab poor, Iraq sought to present the occupation of Kuwait as a cure for social injustice and as the beginning of a new Arab order, in which Iraq would take the lead. Iraq, however, never specified how and when it would initiate the change, and its very call was ridiculed by President Mubarak as hypocrisy.

Aware of the deep-seated anti-imperialist feelings among the Arabs, Iraq presented the US deployment in Saudi Arabia as a new imperialist onslaught on the Arab world, facilitated and encouraged by the Arabs themselves. It portrayed the Saudi decision as an act of betrayal and humiliation of all Arabs, while presenting itself as loyal to the Arab values of dignity, honor, and valor, a country that was still ready to sacrifice its sons in fighting imperialism. Iraq also sought to fire the imagination of the Arabs and Muslims by raising the slogan of liberating Palestine. Saddam Husayn, portrayed as "the new Salah-al-Din," represented the alternative to the policy pursued by Mubarak, who was called "Husni Camp David." Iraq's consistent support of the Palestinian cause was proved, so it claimed, by the fact that Husayn's 12 August initiative gave first priority to the solution of the Palestinian issue. However cynical, manipulative and unrealistic the Palestinian slogan might have appeared to many Arab governments, the Palestinians considered it genuine.

By far the most sustained effort in Iraq's propaganda campaign was the attempt to win Islam to its side. The Islamic symbols and terminology that now permeated Iraqi political discourse were a far cry from the early days of the Ba'th, when this secular party fought relentlessly against any public expression of religiosity. The volte-face was justified by the "war effort," namely the attempt to stop the

US deployment in Saudi Arabia and thwart the Arab-US coalition against Iraq once it had crystallized. The clash was portrayed as one between the true Muslims, represented by Iraq, and the heretics, represented by the US. King Fahd was called a traitor who had facilitated the "invasion" of the holy places by the Americans.

As early as 10 August, Saddam Husayn urged Muslims to "save Mecca and the tomb of the Prophet from occupation."[32] Later, Husayn called for Jihad against the heretics, and the same call was raised by the Islamic congress held in Iraq on 10 August, by the Iraqi National Assembly and by Iraqi 'Ulama, jurists, and preachers. An important symbolic achievement for the Ba'th was a religious ruling (*fatwa*) issued on 18 August by the Grand Shi'i Ayatollah Abu al-Qasim al-Kho'i (of Iranian origin) forbidding "seeking support from heretics against Muslims" and calling on all Muslims to solve their problems peacefully.[33] This was a rare case of Kho'i giving public support to the Ba'th, something he had refused to do during the Iraqi-Iranian War. Nevertheless, he did not call the war a jihad, and in any case, he did not appear to have great influence over the Shi'i 'Ulama and leadership in Iran. Saddam Husayn continued to play the Islamic card for the rest of the year, referring to himself as the descendant of the Prophet Muhammad and to Baghdad as the *qibla* (direction in which Muslims turn when praying) of the mujahidin.[34] his utilization of Islam for political ends mirrored Khomeyni's methods 10 years earlier, except that Husayn had neither the religious authority nor the appeal to carry the masses with him.

Although appealing to Arabs and Muslims in religious terminology made sense, it appeared bizarre when used by Husayn in addressing non-Muslims, as, for example, in a written message to US President Bush and Soviet President Mikhail Gorbachev on the eve of the Helsinki summit on 9 September. In his attempt to

---

32. R. Baghdad, 10 August — DR, 13 August 1990.
33. *Al-Jumhuriyya* (Baghdad), 18 August 1990.
34. R. Baghdad, 23 August — DR, 24 August; *al-Jumhuriyya* (Baghdad), 25 September 1990.

influence their views on Iraq and the occupation of Kuwait, Husayn used a story from Muslim mythology about how God had defeated the Christian Abyssinian Commander Abraha and his troops who had attempted to occupy the Ka'ba more than 1,400 years ago. The story told how God had sent flocks of birds with clay stones (*hijara min sijjil*) in their mouths and feet in order to kill the infidels. Husayn emphasized in his message that the US troops were occupying the land which Abraha had sought to occupy, that the Ka'ba remained sacred to all Muslims, and, therefore, the US-led invasion was directed not only against 200 million Arabs, but also against 1 billion Muslims. Husayn expressed his conviction that God's "virtuous servants" would rise up and resist the invasion, that God would bring them victory and that the Americans' fate would be similar to that of Abraha. He signed the letter "the believing slave of God."[35] The story was repeated by Husayn and the media frequently, and Iraq even decided to name one of its long-range missiles after the *hijara min sijjil*.[36]

No less significant was the fact that one of the many poems written to glorify Husayn after the occupation alluded to him as a prophet: "This one who is living among us has given us the moon and become a prophet."[37] It would appear that during the year Saddam Husayn began to believe that he had a messianic mission to save Arabs and Muslims from the encroachments of the "infidels," and to usher in a new era of Arab and Muslim glory and greatness. Although this self-imposed mission did not give Husayn enough support from the Arab and Muslim public to counterbalance Arab opposition to his policy, the somewhat supranatural element that was infused into Iraqi ideology helps explain his decision to hold onto Kuwait despite the threat of war against a coalition of 28 nations.

35. Iraqi News Agency, 8 September — DR, 10 September 1990.
36. E.g., *al-Thawra* (Baghdad), 9, 10, 12 October 1990; Iraqi News Agency, 31 December 1990 — DR, 3 January 1991.
37. *Alif Ba* (Baghdad), 19 September 1990.

"THE MOTHER OF BATTLES"

After Husayn's rise to power in July 1979, Iraq underwent two diametrically opposed developments: the strengthening of the regime and the weakening of Iraq's society and polity. Political decision-making became limited to the virtually omnipotent ruler and a handful of relatives and close associates, while the involvement of the population or any nongovernmental group in politics became nil. Enfeebled by a decade of intermittent wars, social and economic destruction, and political castration, the population was too weak to resist Husayn's arbitrary decisions or force him to make others that suited its interests. This development became all the more dangerous when Husayn's megalomania led him to apply his domestic style of rule to foreign policy. A similar blurring of boundaries took place between past and present, and between imagination and reality. It is not surprising then that Husayn began to believe that he had a messianic role in history: to revive through Iraqi achievements, the ancient glory of the Arab and Islamic past.

The best shortcut to attain all this was war. But even when "the mother of battles" turned into a terrible military defeat, Husayn still portrayed it as a great Iraqi victory.[38] Thus, he made the Iraqi people the victims of his own propaganda twice over, first by leading them to believe that victory was possible, and then by portraying the worst of defeats as a great victory. Indeed, at no other time in modern Iraqi history has the gap been so wide between lofty talk and bitter reality, which consisted of two consecutive wars in one decade. However, if the yardstick for victory was the survival of Husayn and his regime, then Iraq undoubtedly emerged victorious, no matter what price it had paid.

---

38.   R. Baghdad, 26 February — DR, 26 February 1991.

DOCUMENTS

Editorial Note:
Except where stated otherwise, all documents are taken from the Daily Report (DR):
Middle East and Africa, and monitoring reports published in English translation by
the US Foreign Broadcasting Information Service (FBIS).

1. Saddam Husayn's Speech at the ACC Summit
24 February 1990

Speech by Iraqi President Saddam Husayn at the opening of the fourth summit of the Arab Cooperation Council (ACC) at the Royal Cultural Center in Amman — live. *Amman Television Service in Arabic, 1010 GMT, 24 February 1990.*

In the name of God, the compassionate, the merciful.

Brother heads of the member states of the Arab Cooperation Council (ACC) and members of the ACC Supreme Council, brother King Husayn Bin Talal, brother President Muhammad Husni Mubarak, and brother President 'Ali 'Abdallah Salih, gentlemen, my greetings to you. We meet today in the Arab city of Amman, which is noble by [virtue of] its people and government officials headed by our noble and brave Arab brother His Majesty King Husayn Bin Talal. By our meeting today we inaugurate the second session of our council, just as we inaugurated the first session in Baghdad and followed it up by meetings in Alexandria and San'a.

In this part of Arabdom, where we are enjoying kind, brotherly hospitality among our kinfolk and brothers in blood, Arabism, and common destiny, we have come to carry out a brotherly, pan-Arab role under a formula that has been willed by God and accepted by the righteous sons of this nation. It is a collective, quadripartite formula, unlike those known to the Arab League, bilateral relations, or any other relations established among Arabs under different names in the past.

The first year in the life of our council was a year of foundation and the establishment of the main bases and frameworks for the various fields of cooperation, coordination, and integration among our countries. That year was full of meetings and fruitful achievements. We are entering the second year of the council with this meeting today in Amman and we have great hopes of continuing the march in accordance with the set objectives. We greatly hope that through the determination of His Majesty King Husayn and his brothers in the Jordanian Government, we will continue this march with further determination and resolution to realize even more achievements.

Perhaps the foremost. which we hope to achieve in the current phase is to turn the steps we have taken and the agreements we have signed into tangible facts that can be felt by the people in our countries. Feeling the positive effects and benefits of these steps and agreements will increase our people's enthusiasm for and confidence in the council and its pan-Arab objectives.

Brothers, when we meet in Amman, influenced by pan-Arab slogans, sentiments, and aspirations — after all, this is what unites Arabs everywhere, represents their common aspirations, and makes our meeting here possible, useful, and on the right track — I say, when we meet in Amman, where we can see the bright lights of holy Jerusalem, brotherly and pan-Arab duty makes it incumbent upon us at the outset of this meeting to extend our greetings to the struggling people of Palestine, and to also extend our greetings and gratitude to our brothers in Jordan for their kind hospitality and warm reception which, along with their other kind deeds, affirm their true devotion to Arabism and its objectives.

Despite the difficulty of finding a closer vantage point from which to view the lights of Jerusalem, we see that city from Baghdad through our faithful, penetrating eyes, which have plenty of room for Jerusalem — which, as you well know, has been the scene of great Arab sacrifices and glories, making its name evoke only good memories. We can see Jerusalem from anywhere, no matter how far from that city, because Jerusalem brings out the good things in our hearts. So, the line of sight between us and Jerusalem is straight, thereby shortening the distance between us and that city, and in fact between that city and any Arab, Muslim, or Christian among the sons of Arabism. This makes Jerusalem very close. Thus, the signs on the path of liberating Jerusalem are clear and remain unobliterated by the vicissitudes of time, God willing.

Palestine was usurped through deliberate planning, and it can only be restored through deliberate planning backed by determination to achieve justice. The struggl[ing] sons of Palestine have proved to be an example of determination and readiness for sacrifice. The loss of Palestine was not essentially due to the Zionists' faith in the Zionist cause, but due to the Arabs' abandonment of the Arab cause. It was also not essentially due to Zionist strength, but to Arab weakness. Now that the Arabs have realized — through different factors and reasons, including their triumph over their enemies and the enemies of God on the eastern front and the heroic stand of the people of the deadly stones — that they are capable of taking action, then Palestine will return. Light will chase out darkness and the banners of justice shall fly over holy Jerusalem, God willing.

Brothers, one of the most important and prominent characteristics of this meeting, discussion, and relationship among a small number of Arab League members — as is the case with our meeting today - is that this small number gives us a better chance for analysis and dialogue in a manner that enables us to forge a common stance and a single viewpoint. I think we all agree that our meeting faces a special task of priority, which is indisputable; that is, the discussion and analysis of the changes in the international arena and their repercussions on our countries, on the Arab nation in particular, and on the world in general. This is in addition to the old and new threats to our pan-Arab security. For, since our meeting in Baghdad last February, many phenomena and developments have emerged in the international arena. Some of these are natural, and considered to be recurrent situations that we are familiar with, and some are unfamiliar. To describe some developments as unfamiliar is not only attributable to these developments in themselves, but is also due to their effect on a region that might reflect on the whole globe, positively or negatively. The effect of what happens here or there in all the spots of the globe is no longer confined to a narrow space;

and because the responsibility of enjoying what is positive, or taking measures and precautions against what is negative, is no longer confined to the setting of these events but transcends to nations, whether big or small, it is our duty to study these phenomena and their causes. After we discover the causes, we should interact with the positive aspects so that we can benefit from them. On the other hand, we should take precautions against what is negative through joint positions that will allow the positive aspects to dominate over the negative ones.

Since it is difficult in a meeting such as this to deal with all that is negative or positive in international developments during 1989 and prior to then, and during the period from the beginning of 1990, you might share my opinion that discussions should deal with the most urgent and important of these issues and within the limits of the time allowed us.

Among the most important developments since the international conflict in World War II has been the fact that some countries which used to enjoy broad international influence, such as France and Britain, have declined, while the influence and impact of two countries expanded until they became the two superpowers among the countries of the world — I mean the United States and the Soviet Union. Of course, with these results, two axes have developed: the Western axis under the leadership of the United States, with its known capitalist approach and its imperialist policy; [and] the Eastern Bloc under the leadership of the Soviet Union and its communist philosophy.

Among the results of World War II, the Zionist state has become a reality, and the original owners of the land, the Palestinians, have become refugees. While the imperialist Western world helped the expansionist scheme and aggression of the Zionist entity in 1967, the communist bloc sided with the Arabs in the concept of balance of interests in the context of the global competition between the two blocs, and sought to secure footholds for the Eastern Bloc against the Western interests in the Arab homeland. The Eastern bloc, led by the USSR, supported the Arabs' basic rights, including their rights in the Arab-Zionist conflict. The global policy continued on the basis of the existence of two poles that were balanced in terms of force. They are the two superpowers, the United States and the USSR.

And suddenly, the situation changed in a dramatic way. The USSR turned to tackle its domestic problems after relinquishing the process of continuous conflict and its slogans. The USSR shifted from the balanced position with the United States in a practical manner, although it has not acknowledged this officially so far. The USSR went to nurse the wounds that were inflicted on it as a result of the principles and the mistaken policy it followed for such a long time, and as a result of the wave of change it embarked on, which began to depart from the charted course. It has become clear to everyone that the United States has emerged in a superior position in international politics. This superiority will be demonstrated in the US readiness to play such a role more than in the predicted guarantees for its continuation.

We believe that the world can fill the vacuum resulting from the recent changes and find a new balance in the global arena by developing new perspectives and reducing or adding to this or that force. The forces that laid the ground for filling the vacuum and for the emergence of the two superpowers, the US and the USSR, after World War II at the expense of France, Britain, and Germany, can develop new forces, which we expect will be in Europe and Japan. America will lose its power just as quickly as it gained it by frightening Europe, Japan, and other countries through the continuous hinting at the danger of the USSR and communism. The United States will lose its power as the fierce competition for gaining the upper hand between the two superpowers and their allies recedes.

However, we believe that the US will continue to depart from the restrictions that govern the rest of world throughout the next five years until new forces of balance are formed. Moreover, the undisciplined and irresponsible behavior will engender hostility and grudges if it embarks on rejected stupidities.

Given the relative erosion of the role of the Soviet Union as the key champion of the Arabs in the context of the Arab-Zionist conflict and globally, and given that the influence of the Zionist lobby on US policies is as powerful as ever, the Arabs must take into account that there is a real possibility that Israel might embark on new stupidities within the five-year span I have mentioned. This might take place as a result of direct or tacit US encouragement. On the other hand, the Arabs have a plus, and that is Arab solidarity that will be effective if the Arabs work out a well-defined plan of action and devise regional policies *vis-à-vis* neighboring foreign countries, and if they forge fruitful cooperation based on strong foundations oriented toward clear goals. The cooperation will have to encompass culture, politics, economics, and other areas. Recent American utterances and behavior as far as pan-Arab security and Palestinian Arab rights to their homeland are concerned inevitably cause alarm and warrant Arab vigilance, or are supposed to evoke such a reaction on our part. One may cite recurrent statements by US officials about their intention to keep their fleets in the Gulf for an unlimited period of time, and their support for an unprecedented exodus of Soviet Jews to Palestinian territory, neither of which would have been possible solely under cover of the human rights slogan had not the Americans put pressure on the Soviets, exploiting the latter's special circumstances so as to incorporate the issue into their bilateral agreements with the Soviets. Add to that the increasing support for the Zionist entity's strategic arms stockpiles and giving it license to deploy them when necessary, the judgment on when to use them being left up to Israel. This is above and beyond US assistance to Israel in other areas.

We all remember, as does the whole world, the circumstances under which the United States deployed and bolstered its fleets in the Gulf. Most important of these circumstances: The war that was raging between Iraq and Iran. Iranian aggression had extended to other Arabian Gulf countries, most notably the sisterly state of Kuwait. At the time, beyond the conflicting views regarding the presence of foreign fleets in Arab territorial waters and foreign bases on their territory and their repercussions for pan-Arab security, that excessive deployment was somehow comprehensible. But now, and against the background of the recent world developments and the cessation of hostilities between Iraq and Iran, and with Kuwait no longer being the target of Iranian aggression, the Arabian Gulf states, including Iraq, and even the entire Arab [world] would have liked the Americans to state their intention to withdraw their fleets.

Had they said that under the same circumstances and causes they would have returned to the Gulf, it might have been understandable also. But US officials are making such statements as if to show that their immediate and longer-term presence in Gulf waters, and maybe on some of its territory, is not bound to a time frame. These suspect policies give Arabs reason to feel suspicious of US policies and intentions as to whether it is officially and actually interested in a termination of the Iraq-Iran war and thus contribute to much needed regional stability.

The other side is the immigration of Soviet Jews to the occupied Palestinian land. How can we explain the Americans' support and backing for Jewish immigration to the occupied Arab territories, except that the United States does not want peace as it claims and declares. If it really and actually wanted peace, the United States would not encourage Israel and the aggressive trends in it to adopt such policies, which enhance Israel's capability to commit aggression and carry out expansion.

We, the Arabs, proceeding from a long-standing friendship with the Soviet Union, did not expect that the Soviets would give in to this US pressure in such a way that it would lead to these grave consequences for the Arabs and their pan-Arab security. As we tackle these challenges, it would be just as compromising to the destiny and cause of the Arabs to feel fear as it would be to be lax in our evaluating and working out a reaction to them. Therefore, there is no place among the ranks of good Arabs for the fainthearted who would argue that as a superpower, the United States will be the decisive factor, and others have no choice but to submit. At the same time, there is no place in our midst for those who fail to take note of recent developments that have added to US strength, thus prompting it to the possible commission of follies against the interests and national security of the Arabs — either directly or by fanning and encouraging conflicts detrimental to the Arabs, irrespective of their source. We are not thus out to antagonize or to incite public opinion against the United States on the strength of mere speculation over potential developments. We are only making the point that the Arabs seek peace and justice throughout the world and want to forge relations of friendship with those who show respect to what friendship is all about — be it the United States or any other nation. It is only natural that the Arabs take a realistic approach to the new posture and power of the United States that has led the Soviet Union to abandon its erstwhile position of influence. However, America must respect the Arabs and respect their rights, and should not interfere in their internal affairs under any cover. The United States must not forget that the Arab nation is a great nation that taught humanity things it had been ignorant of. Otherwise, there is no room for unilateral friendship or unilateral respect, and there will be no consideration for the interests and rights of any party unless it is capable of understanding and respecting the Arabs' rights, interests, dignity, options, and pan-Arab security. Against the backdrop of the vital issues related to the substance of national Arab security, the question arises as to what we, the Arabs, have to do.

One of certain indisputable things, brothers, is that the correct description for a certain situation is not necessarily the correct solution to that situation, but an inevitable introduction leading to the correct solution. Therefore, in all cases, a solution does not merely consist of defining which issues are rejected, both concerning our behavior or the behavior and thinking of others who harm our pan-Arab security and national and pan-Arab interests. Another thing over which there is no room for dispute is that the policy of the age is not set by concerned foreign parties on any basis other than policies and strategies whose expected final result is to serve the interests of their countries.

Zionism realized these facts and concentrated its international effort here and there in accordance with an accurate perception and longer-lasting knowledge than that of the Arabs. The Zionists were progressive initiators in fields where they would disrupt the calculations and influences of the Arabs. In accordance with this basis, and not only on the basis of developing public opinion, Zionism directed its special concentration on the United States of America to involve it in its strategy, after realizing that the future of its goals and joint action with the Europeans would come up against special obstacles. The United States accepted the concept of joining interests and action with Zionism out of its concept of its own interests, after the United States had taken over the role of the European colonialists following World War II.

Despite all the harm the United States inflicted upon the Arabs due to its alliance with Zionism, there remained the fear of communism, the Soviet Union, and the Arab friends and allies of the Soviet Union in the region, in addition to other factors. This continued to prevent the Arabs from taking influential stands towards US policy, with minor exceptions. Their stands became restricted to a mere ineffective rejection or an ineffective silence and acceptance. The United States began not to take Arab stances seriously. The United States may have the famous red lines beyond which it does not tread concerning the interests of other nations that deal peacefully with it, but its policy so far has no red lines warning the concerned sides in the United States not to tread beyond them where Arab interests are concerned.

Realizing Arab solidarity on the basis of pan-Arab interests, correctly defining Arab interests, clearly and accurately defining everything that threatens their security and stability, and proceeding from this basis of capability, frankness, and solidarity with the United States, or other countries in general, prevents these countries from exceeding the proper bounds with the Arab nation and thus becoming a threat.

This might be a realistic basis for the establishment of Arab relations with the United States and other states, based on the principles I have mentioned. These are mutual respect, noninterference in internal affairs, and respect for the requirements of pan-Arab security and common interests on a legitimate and agreed-upon basis.

Brothers, Zionism and its entity, Israel, have been used to embark upon areas and affairs to which the Arabs do not pay attention. The Arabs have also been used on occasion to rise all together to counter the Zionists' political, informational, or any other offensive for which Zionism has prepared all requirements through effective work over a long period of time. The Arabs would launch a counteroffensive without being fully prepared and soon their rising would dwindle and vanish. Therefore, the Arab reaction is often verbal or ineffective even if part of it takes the form of real action. In politics as well as in war, responsibility and experience have taught us that the counteroffensive should not necessarily be on the same axis that is always chosen by the enemy, especially when the encounter lasts a long time and when it is possible to choose one or more axes or one or more places other than those from which the enemy began its offensive and for which it prepared the requirements of confrontation and took into consideration Arab reaction. In such a case it might be enough to preoccupy the enemy on the axis selected for its offensive against us, and then we would attack it from another axis if the desired results were possible on the other axis. Accordingly, the direct offensive on the harmful plans and means used by the US and Zionism against the Arabs in a certain field might not always be the right solution if we use all of our potential at one time in a manner that takes us away from other fields.

The big does not become big nor does the great earn such a description unless he is in the arena of comparison or fighting with someone else on a different level. The big powers become big only when small and medium-sized countries were found on this earth around these big powers. The big powers do not become big unless they are influential in small and medium-sized countries. Accordingly, among the means to weaken hostile policies and the harmful influence of those who harm us is to weaken the one who harms us inside or outside his national soil. Accordingly, and because interest is the basis of the Soviet Union's new policy, as well as the policy of the East European states, as it has always been the basis of the policy of other states, we are dutybound to ask and answer accurately how we can approach these states in order to weaken our enemies' influence on them or how we can benefit from our common financial, economic, political, informational, and other powers to achieve better results.

It has been proven that Arabs are capable of being influential when they make a decision and set their minds to it for actual application purposes. We have much evidence of how effective they can be. For example, the joint Iraqi-Saudi resolution of 6 August 1980, and the warning the two countries issued together that embassies must not be moved to Jerusalem, one of whose direct results in less than a month — the duration of the warning — was not only that the concerned countries did not transfer their embassies to Jerusalem, but also that embassies that had already long been transferred to the city returned to Tel Aviv.

The reason the United States stays in the Gulf is that the Gulf has become the most important spot in the region and perhaps the whole world due to developments in international policy, the oil market, and increasing demands from the United States, Europe, Japan, Eastern Europe, and perhaps the Soviet Union, for this product. The country that will have the greatest influence in the region through the Arab Gulf and its oil will maintain its superiority as a superpower without an equal to compete with it. This means that if the Gulf people, along with all Arabs, are not careful, the Arab Gulf region will be governed by the US will. If the Arabs are not alerted and the weakness persists, the situation could develop to the extent desired by the United States; that is, it would fix the amount of oil and gas produced in each country and sold to this or that country in the world. Prices would also be fixed in line with a special perspective benefiting US interests and ignoring the interests of others.

If this possibility is there and it is convincing, those who are convinced by it must conclude that peace in the Middle East is remote from the US point of view because US strategy, according to this analysis, needs an aggressive Israel, not a peaceful one. Peace between Iraq and Iran could be far off as long as Iran does not react favorably from an aware and responsible position and with the peace initiatives proposed by Iraq. The region could witness inter-

Arab wars or controlled wars between the Arabs and some of their neighbors, if tangible results are not achieved on the basis of the principles of noninterference in others' internal affairs and nonuse of military force in inter-Arab relations.

Agreement should be reached over clear and widespread pan-Arab cooperation programs among Arab countries in the economic, political, and educational fields, as well as other fields. Love and peace of mind will take the place of suspicion, doubt, mistrust, and giving in to information and speculation propagated by rumormongers such as prejudiced Westerners and some rootless Arabs.

Brothers, the weakness of a big body lies in its bulkiness. All strong men have their Achilles' heel. Therefore, irrespective of our known stand on terror and terrorists, we saw that the United States as a superpower departed Lebanon immediately when some Marines were killed, the very men who are considered to be the most prominent symbol of its arrogance. The whole US Administration would have been called into question had the forces that conquered Panama continued to be engaged by the Panamanian Armed Forces. The United States has been defeated in some combat arenas for all the forces it possesses, and it has displayed signs of fatigue, frustration, and hesitation when committing aggression on other peoples' rights and acting from motives of arrogance and hegemony. This is a natural outcome for those who commit aggression on other peoples' rights. Israel, once dubbed the invincible country, has been defeated by some of the Arabs. The resistance put up by Palestinian and Lebanese militia against Israeli invasion forces in 1982 and before that the heroic Egyptian crossing of the Suez Canal in 1973 have had a more telling psychological and actual impact than all Arab threats. Further, the threat to use Arab oil in 1973 during the October war proved more effective than all political attempts to protest or to beg at the gates of American decision-making centers. The stones in occupied Palestine now turn into a virtual and potentially fatal bullet if additional requirements are made available. It is the best proof of what is possible and indeed gives us cause to hold our heads high.

Just as Israel controls interests to put pressure on the US Administration, hundreds of billions invested by the Arabs in the United States and the West may be similarly deployed. Indeed, for instance, some of these investments may be diverted to the USSR and East European countries. It may prove even more profitable than investment in the West, which has grown saturated with its national resources. Such a course of action may yield inestimable benefits for the Arabs and their national causes.

Our purported weakness does not lie in our ideological and hereditary characteristics. Contemporary experience has shown our nation to be distinguished and excellent, just as our nation's history over the centuries has shown this to be the case. Our purported weakness lies in a lack of mutual trust among ourselves, our failure to concentrate on the components of our strength, and our failure to focus on our weaknesses with a view to righting them. Let our motto be: All of us are strong as long as we are united, and all of us are weak as long as we are divided. Then we will see how all of us will reach safe shores, God willing, so we can take off together on the road of stability and prosperity, heartening our people and ourselves. We will also see how Satan will grow weaker wherever he may be and the evil will depart our homeland and our nation. We are proceeding with resolve and firmness, God willing, to reach this goal through brotherly cooperation that would serve as a model for common Arab action and developed brotherly cooperation. Let us go forward.

Brother leaders of the ACC countries, brother members of the audience, these are ideas and concepts that we are proposing for brotherly dialogue in the context of an exchange of views and experience among us on all issues of concern to our Arab countries and nation. We ask success from God toward the good. The peace and blessings of God be upon you, brothers.

Source: FBIS-NES-90-039, 27 February 1990.

2. President Warns Israel, Criticizes US
1 April 1990

"Full recording" of a speech by President Saddam Husayn at a ceremony honoring the minister of defense, the minister of industry and military industrialization, and members of the Armed Forces General Command, on 1 April 1990 (place not given) — recorded. *Baghdad Domestic Service in Arabic 1030 GMT, 2 April 1990.*

God be praised for everything. God be praised because Iraq has remained safe. God be praised that with God's safety, the nation is now in a new condition. Had it not been for this outcome, or had the outcome been the opposite, things would have been very bad. Things would have been so bad that we would not be able to imagine them or picture their form.

The main pillar of this glory, at the forefront of those who built this main pillar, are the martyrs, who are more honorable than any of us. These martyrs are followed by the men who are on the level of these martyrs, despite the fact that we cannot define very clear limits for that. The men who were placed on the path of the martyrs are also on the same level of the martyrs when judged by the outcome. This is because when God almighty spared them, he intended to realize something through his will and wisdom. Likewise, God willed that some become martyrs.

Did the attempts end when victory was realized? The central pillar of the conspiracy was certainly broken because no bigger conspiracy could be imagined. I can say this before the Iraqis because I do not tell the Iraqis anything unless it is repeatedly settled in my mind and unless my conscience is satisfied with it. Only when my conscience is satisfied with it will I tell them about it. The conspiracy, whose central pillar the Iraqis have broken, will never occur again, not in our time and not in times to come. This is the biggest conspiracy in modern history, until God might accomplish a matter already enacted [Koranic phrase]. However, the flames of fire will not end.

In the past, they tried to push the Iraqis away from the path of light but now have realized that the Iraqis have wielded the path of light and covered a distance on it. Now the attempts, as you might describe them, are attempts to place impediments. They wager on time, as the original players in the big conspiracy wagered. These players from outside the region were wagering on time, and this is one of the things with which they used to delude the Iranians and force them to make mistakes. This forced the two countries to make sacrifices. Iraq made sacrifices and the Iranians suffered losses. From the very beginning and from their first attempts, when they started to feel the pulse and to attack, and when they were faced with the well-known resistance, it was clear to them — it was supposed to have been clear — that the time that they had in mind was not the time of this age. This time, on which they base their judgment and during which they hope to realize certain results, will not materialize.

Had they realized this, they would have spared themselves, their country, and their people many disasters and spared our country and people many sacrifices. However, God almighty wanted this to happen.

I say that hurling darts of fire at Iraq, as our people in the countryside describe them, will not cease. The main players in the past during the war used to play the game through Iran, but now, after the great result that has been realized, they find that they have no choice but to play the game themselves. The big ones, therefore, are now playing the game directly. They have found that the Iraqis have set their feet firmly on the path of light in the direction of the objectives they set for themselves. The objectives are a life of happiness and prosperity for the Iraqis and for Iraq to become a strong support for the Arab nation in defense of its rights, security, and sanctities.

Our duty here is the same as of those who carry the al-Qadisiyya Sword and take the oath of national duty you have just heard. In other words, we have a duty to defend Iraq. We must defend it without expecting any favor in return and without anyone reminding us of our duty. The nature of the current phase and the principles we uphold say that if an Arab, wherever he may be, from the East to the Maghreb, is exposed to a foreign aggression, and this Arab permits us to defend his rights against a foreign occupier or usurper, it is our duty to do that. Is there anything wrong with that? Are we committing aggression against anyone by doing that? No, we are not. This is our country and Iraq's map is well known. A foreigner must not attack the Arab homeland.

We are not carrying the banner of challenge. We are not challenging anyone. But if anyone challenges us, he will find us more solid than a diamond, delicate but also firm. We cannot be trampled on. We are not pushovers. By we I mean all of us, not just this speaker. Many of you may be stronger physically, and firmer than this speaker. I will not say that you are firmer than this speaker on rights, since I may not be accurate. At any rate, we are all one man as far as defending rights. God bless you, you are youthful and strong. True, some of you are stronger than I and Abu Muthanna (referring to someone in the audience), but when it comes to fighting, each one will do his best. Fighting does not call for strong muscles, but a strong heart first and the rest depends on God. Isn't this so, (Information Minister) Latif?

We have not and we will not commit aggression against anyone, but everybody is looking at the Iraqi borders as they are now drawn. The drone which dares to approach these borders or commits aggression on Iraq, will have its sting cut off from behind and its head cut off from the front. We will leave only the middle part. If an aggression is committed against an Arab and that Arab seeks our assistance from afar, we will not fail to come to his assistance, God willing. If they want to record this stand against Iraq, let them do so right now. We are not different from others. Was the Arab born to be trampled on by others? What injustice! Fear God. After all, who are the banner-carriers? Should anyone be surprised by the Iraqis defending their borders and land? Why are the Americans and English surprised because the Iraqis are defending their homeland and triumphing? When Baghdad was overrun [by the Tatars] in

1258 and the Iraqis were hit on the head, ending their glory, that did not represent their true state.

These are passing circumstances for Iraqis. They have to familiarize themselves with Baghdad in the times when it was the foremost radiating center in the world and they were living in caves, when some of them were gangs invading America from all corners of the globe. They set out with bands of murderers who assembled in America, but present-day America is a great nation — a great nation by material standards not by moral standards. A great person is judged by his manners. The United States is a superpower in accordance with material yardsticks. It is not a superpower in accordance with moral and ethical yardsticks. The great are great in terms of ethics, and the United States will become a superpower and enter our hearts and minds when it acts in a true ethical and legal manner. A country becomes great on the basis of its ethical leverage, that is, when it sponsors the rights of people and nations, when it defends the principles of international law, and when it defends all causes, not merely certain selected ones.

They may think that Saddam Husayn is upset by their propaganda, but I am not. However, I would like to point out to them what is right and what is wrong. The reason is that usually only a few in the world have pointed out to them what is right and what is wrong. The smallest state, no matter how small its territory or population (changes thought).... Considering that we are a state 17 million strong — what do you think, Latif? (chuckles) Please sit down. Considering that we are a state 17 million strong and our territory is relatively small (changes thought)....But they (word indistinct) they must not belittle our valleys. Our valleys are legion. In this good assembly chests are studded with decorations, medals and swords. Certainly there will be more swords as called for by the recent decision when the swords (word indistinct) by the Presidential Office.

Yesterday, I was talking to the minister of agriculture and repeated what I told him to the governors when they were sworn in. I told them that weakness and strength are judged by two yardsticks: right and injustice. Whom do we fear? We fear God and our people. We fear God because we are believers, thanks be to God. We fear our people when we take a route they disapprove of. In other words, we monitor our route lest we go astray and our people are alienated. We hold our people dearly. Our fear is not technical, it is humanitarian based on solidarity with our people, because we love our people. We take pains not to upset our people through anything we do. We fear only these two: God and our people. We are prepared to carry our people on our shoulders in the manner of a dutiful son carrying his parents in their old age when they are not able to move about. We carry our people on our shoulders without feeling the weight. This is to guard against a day when we may have to carry foreigners on our shoulders. Should anyone fail to carry his people, the foreigner will do the job for him.

Our carrying our people is not an invention. If anyone wants to carry someone else, he will tire quickly. He will let him down every once in a while. We learned it long ago when we were in secondary school.

If our people are at ease and we are not opposed to justice — we are not opposed to international humanitarian practices — then why should we be afraid? If the strongest force in the world confronts us with injustice, we will fight back with the old woman from the Hindiyya region. We fight back with the old woman from the Hindiyya region, the one who is 100 years old and tells Saddam Husayn not to fear, we are your right hand. Did you see her on television? She is 100 years old and has so much confidence that it makes you want to move toward the fire. One hundred years old and yet she tells Saddam Husayn not to be afraid because we are your right hand. Fear no one. Truly, truly, in faith we hope to God that we will not fear anyone but God, because our people support us in our justice.

Why are the main players so upset? Could they not have stopped the war in eight years? Do we not know that? They can stop whatever they want in weeks or even days. But they let Iraq and Iran fight for eight years. And the fighting took place on the brink of the well in which 65 per cent of the world's oil reserves are found. At the brink of this well the fighting and shelling took place, while they say:

no problem (preceding two words in English), as they say in English
— no problem. They are the no-problem people.
For eight years, they have been quite satisfied and pleased with us
just to sell us weapons and bring down the price of oil. In eight years,
they brought it down to seven dollars. They also brought down the
dollar value for the oil-producing people so that they could get less
cash, one-third the price. They played these games for eight years
and just let the Iraqis fight for their rights. They would give Iraq
something and then conspire to give al-Faw to Iran, though they
knew that we would die rather than suffer the occupier. They
conspired against us in 1986 and raised the al-Faw issue.

The great players have now entered the arena with all their might.
We are not awed by them. We fear no one when right is on our side.
We fear only God and that is because God is justice. Let those who
want to occupy Iraq try to do it. Let them come. These are the ports
of southern Iraq. Let them come and may God help them.

Let our people continue to wear the best clothes. Khaki is a nice
and good color and we will continue to wear it for 1,000 years. If
they do not want us to wear civilian clothing, then we will not do so.
It is no problem. Our people wear civilian clothing when they are
relaxed and feel protected, with God's help.

Why are they so disturbed? The Israeli, US and British intelligence
services have been trying for the past five or six years to pass
enriched uranium to us. They used to come to us every day and tell
us: Don't you want enriched uranium to produce an atomic bomb?
By God, spare us your evil. Pick up your goods and leave. We do not
need an atomic bomb. We have the binary chemical (*al-kimawi
al-muzdawij*). Let them take not of this. We have the binary
chemical. According to our information only the United States and
the Soviet Union have it. They still have not reached an agreement
with respect to its disarmament. It exists in Iraq. So that the Iraqis
may know, it existed during the last period of the war — I believe
during the last year of the war. It was there. In spite of this, we did
not use it against the Iranians. We did not use it against the Iranians.
We said that the weapons we had were more than enough, and
hoped that God would enable us to liberate our land without it.

Why, then, do we need the atomic bomb? Do they know that the capacitors that are worth only $10,500 do not produce atomic bombs? Don't they know the facts? Are they not ashamed of their white hair? Is Thatcher not ashamed of her white hair? Are the others, including the Americans, not ashamed of their white hair when they talk about capacitors costing $10,500, whose use and purposes are well-known? They transformed these into nuclear trigger devices and said that Iraq now possesses nuclear bombs, which is something new to them. How can this be while you claim that you know everything that takes place in the world?

See how disturbed they are? I have told you that this is perhaps the fourth or fifth year, and some of these offers had been made to us before the war. They offered us uranium before the war, and asked us whether we wanted to purchase it. By God, we do not want uranium. What shall we do with it? The British, US, and Zionist intelligence sent them (nuclear trigger devices) so as to say: See, Iraq is producing a nuclear bomb. This is the policy of entrapment. When a country is in a state of war, and someone comes and says: Let me sell you...One of them said: We have a nuclear bomb if you want to purchase it. Take a country that is in a state of war and whose territory is occupied, and nuclear bombs do exist in the word (sentence as heard). They are there and are not banned. The Americans, the Soviets and others have it. This being the case, someone comes and tells you: I have a nuclear weapon which I want to sell you. Had the Iraqis not been wise and balanced and enjoyed a sense of responsibility, they would have told him: Give me this nuclear bomb. This is the policy of entrapment. Is this the right policy with which the real intentions of others are tested?

This is a policy which is similar to that which some security organs used to use at the beginning of the revolution when they suspected that someone was working against the revolution. They used to send some people to those whom they suspected to propose to him to join a hostile party. When I came to know about this I told the people concerned: Should we nòt try to convince these people who have bad intentions to change their course with good words and not try to entrap them? Is this what the superpower's honor and sense of responsibility means, that it resorts to the method of entrapment against the other party? Thanks be to God, in spite of this entrapment method, we were not enticed by their suspicious offers. You will soon read about the details of how they have tried time and again. The issue revolves around the purchase of the capacitors from the local American market at the price of $10,500. Thanks be to God, they have nothing else on us. Each of these capacitors which they claim can produce a nuclear bomb costs only $100. They created a big uproar about Bazoft. Therefore, the new slogan of human rights that the big powers are upholding is to protect the spies. By God, we will cut the spy who comes to Iraq into four pieces. Let those who want to listen take note of this. Those who have spies here, let them remove them (applause). This country belongs to the Iraqis, the Arabs, and to those who enter Iraq peacefully, as friends, whether they be American, French, German, or Soviet. If they enter Iraq peacefully, we welcome them. All the doors of Iraq will be open.

But the one who comes to Iraq as a spy, thinking that he is being backed by a big power, should know that here in Iraq there are no big powers. In Iraq there are national Iraqi standards. A big power is most welcome when it is right: it is smaller than an ant when based on falsehood. This is our law. This is how we are. If they accept us, accordingly we will be their friends. If they try any other method, they will reap nothing. They will only be wasting their time for nothing at all.

We have not held out with all the Iraqis. The Iraqi Kurds have come now. Not all the Kurds of Iraq were among the good ones who fought. Now they will all fight, all the Kurds of Iraq, from one extreme end of Kurdistan to the other. I tell you most assuredly that they will all, like you fight in defense of the land because they have discovered the extent of the defect which had to be discovered. They also discovered the right way of becoming one hand. The son of al-'Amara and the son of al-Sulaymaniyya became one hand; the son of Irbil and the son of al-Anbar became one hand; and Iraq is for all.

Therefore, when they found that the small players could bring about no result, the major ones themselves appeared, with their image and gray hair. We want to be friends with all those who befriend us without exception. But we will not regret being unable to befriend anyone who tries to antagonize us. God willing, the Iranians will discover the facts. Now they have discovered the bitter facts. They will further discover how much they were manipulated into this war and how many life opportunities their people have missed. The one who seeks a calm and stable life for his people can do so only through peace. Peace does not cost much. The price of peace is only having intentions for peace. The one who has a will for peace will reach peace. The peace Iraq is proposing does not contain an encroachment on rights nor an attempt to violate the rights of anyone. But it is at the same time the peace through which Iraq will not allow anyone to violate rights, in the same way that Iraq did not allow the war to violate these rights.

They are talking about Bazoft's rights. Are the Palestinians not human beings? They are talking about Bazoft's rights while the suspect newspapers continue to write about a German scientist, claiming that he was cooperating with Iraq. [An unidentified person is heard correcting the president by telling him the scientist, Gerald Bull, is Canadian, not German.] He is a Canadian with US nationality. Just imagine this international hypocrisy. Although you, the military are aware of the target entrusted to you, it would not hurt to explain to you an aspect of this international hypocrisy. A Canadian citizen with US nationality came to Iraq. He is a scientist too. He might have benefited Iraq, I do not know. They say the Iraqi intelligence service is spread in Europe — [Kamil] Husayn's industry intelligence. That is what they say. But nobody spoke about the human rights of this Canadian citizen of US nationality, while there was [a] hue and cry about Bazoft, who had no British nationality, only documents.

This Canadian...what's his name? (someone in the audience calls out the name.) Whatever. This naturalized American. Is he not entitled to human rights? When he came to Iraq, they killed him. They killed him with a silencer-equipped pistol. As far as they are concerned, he was not entitled to human rights, although he was American. Why was he not entitled to human rights? This is because he was not fit to be used to promote a presidential candidate in the United States. We therefore see only that part of their extremism on human rights in which we believe and urge that they be honored anywhere in the world. But in practice, they are hypocrites. They are using it as a slogan for neo-imperialism, for meddling in the internal affairs of others.

The US intelligence services have not bothered to uncover the murderer of this American scientist. But they create a fuss about other things. Why did the English not remember human rights when they partitioned Palestine and led us to this result? Only now do they remember human rights — regarding the spy Bazoft. The English have not spared a nation on earth from their problems. They charted maps and left things unsettled to create problems. Only Bazoft is a human being. They see Bazoft as a human being. But when Bazoft passes intelligence to the Zionist entity in order for it to accurately hit a plant and kill maybe 200 or 300 people...these do not count as human beings. Only Bazoft is a human being, and the 17 million have no right to defend themselves.

Look, Iraqis and Arabs, look at how you are regarded. You are not considered human beings. Only their agents and spies are looked upon as humans. According to them, they are more entitled to rights than an entire people or nation. Let losers be disappointed. If some imagine that this clamor will intimidate us, an old woman in al-Hindiyya told us not to worry. When they convince the 100-year-old woman in al-Hindiyya and the 100-year-old man in Nineve that we will be afraid, then we may debate the question. So let's forget about fear. How can an official feel fear? It's a shame. An official may be cautious and be on his guard, but at the same time he will keep in mind his people's and country's dignity. He will remember that a 100-year-old woman of his people — one among tens of thousands her age, aside from the younger people — tells Saddam Husayn not to worry. Never worry, Saddam Husayn, we are your support. If 100-year-olds tell Saddam Husayn not to worry, is there anyone left who will be afraid? How then shall we feel fear? They will be deluded if they imagine that they can give Israel a cover in order to come and strike at some industrial metalworks. By God, we will make fire eat up half of Israel if it tried [anything) against Iraq.

Everyone must know his limits. Thanks be to God, we know our limits and we will not attack anyone. Neither will we become conceited or forget our humanitarian responsibility, or our national and pan-Arab responsibilities. However, the others must also not forget their humanitarian responsibilities. Anyone who tries to belittle Iraq — and we will not say any more than what we have said — will have only himself to blame. This time we will deal with them in this way.

With God's help and with the courage of Iraqis — and when I say Iraqis, I mean Iraqi men and women, old and young — all eyes are open. Thanks be to God. He gave the Iraqis clever minds, with which to think well. And when we go to sleep, we sleep with one eye open.

In 1981, I made a speech someplace. The speech was recorded, and the media can refer to it. I told Israel that we know that you want to prolong this war, but the day will come when you will feel sorry for prolonging this war. I said something like that; I cannot remember very well. Did we want this war, did we want it to go on for so long? They made it, they prolonged it, and they are sorry for its results. What can we do? We are a people who want to live in dignity, and who have the right to live in dignity.

They learned their first lessons in humanity and science from Baghdad. All of their discoveries, which they are proud of now and which they deny the Arabs — particularly the Arabs — and Iraq the right of benefiting from in the international and humanitarian sciences, they have learned all this, and the first lesson in science, from Baghdad. Do people with a 6,000-year-old and deep-rooted civilization have the right to live in dignity? Yes, they have the right to live in dignity.

O God, stop the excessiveness of the reckless and unjust people. We will say no more than what our forefathers have said: Give us a strong back, not a light weight. With God's grace the Iraqis will cling to the rays of sun and light wherever there is sun. No power on earth can make them let go of the rays of sunlight or the decent, dignified, calm, and proud life.

Convey my greetings, greetings of men, to all men in the armed forces, and to all men in the regiments of national security from Kurdistan to al-Faw. Thank you, brothers.

Source: FBIS-NES-90-064, 3 April 1990.

3. Saddam Husayn Addresses Visiting US Senators 12 April 1990

"Full text" of President Saddam Husayn's remarks during a meeting with a delegation of US senators led by Robert Dole in Mosul on 12 April 1990 — read by announcer. *Baghdad Domestic Service in Arabic 1400 GMT, 16 April 1990.*

The president: You are welcome.

Senator Dole: At 2300 we had a telephone conversation with the President; we each talked to him. President Bush was satisfied with our plans to visit Baghdad. Your Excellency the President, we would like to present a letter to you signed by the five of us. We have also provided the interpreter with a copy. We hope we will be able to talk with Your Excellency after the letter is read. It is a short letter.

(The interpreter reads the letter:) Your Excellency President Saddam Husayn, Baghdad, Dear Mr. President: We appreciate your readiness to receive us in the blessed month of Ramadan on such short notice. Our delegation to Baghdad represents the two political parties in the United States because we believe Iraq is playing a major role in the Middle

East. As we desire to improve relations between our two countries, it is clear to us we cannot resolve the existing serious differences between our two countries if we neglect these differences or fail to benefit from the opportunity to conduct clear and frank talks.

We therefore believe we have to tell you about our very deep concern over certain policies and activities by your government which represent a big obstacle to developed relations between our two countries.

Your country emerged recently from a lengthy and costly war, which caused concern about the security of your country. But we will not dwell on our belief that your attempts to develop nuclear, chemical, and biological capabilities will expose your country to a serious danger instead of reinforcing that security. Moreover, these attempts will threaten other countries in the region and will cause serious trouble throughout the Middle East. Your recent statements, in which you threatened to use chemical weapons against Israel, have created deep concern in countries all over the world, and it is good for you and for peace in the Middle East to urge you to reconsider going ahead with these dangerous programs, statements, and provocative assertions. We also have to express our deep concern over the alleged activities that led to the expulsion of a member of your diplomatic mission at the United Nations on charges he was involved in murder. Therefore, we reiterate that if we want better relations for our countries, such activities as alleged should not recur.

Finally, we urge Your Excellency to actively and constructively contribute to the current peace process involving Egypt, Israel, and representatives of the Palestinian people and the US Government. Your Excellency, we thank you again for receiving us, and we are looking forward to exchanging views and ideas today.

(Signed) Senator Robert Dole, Senator Simpson, Senator McClure, and Senator Metzenbaum.

Delegation member: Your Excellency the President, the five of us who make up the delegation are prominent members of the US Congress. If we add together the years of experience of the five of us in Congress, they will come to 75 years. Therefore, we have long experience.

We consider this visit very important. During his telephone conversation with us yesterday, President George Bush said we wanted to improve relations with your country and your government. As we stated in the letter, there are grave factors of concern. We also know you have your own concerns.

We were told by President Mubarak and King Husayn that we could hold a frank and open dialogue with you, that you are a clear and a frank man, and that you would explain your ideas. Therefore, as I told the foreign minister before we met you, we want to know what we can do to improve our relations. I briefed the foreign minister on two press reports, the first, by the NBC television network, concerning biological weapons. It is a lengthy report on your capabilities in the field of germ warfare. The second report appeared this morning and refers to some congressmen calling for sanctions against Iraq. Despite this (as heard), it is fair to say that in light of recent media reports, the talk about sanctions again will come up when the Congress resumes its sessions next week. Finally, I would like to borrow words from Senator Specter, whom you met and who went away with a very positive impression of you.

The president: Convey my greetings to him. My impression of him also was good, and he was fair.

Senator Dole: In fact, Senator Specter said that before anything else, we should talk with President Saddam Husayn. He urged the other congressmen to show self-restraint in this respect. I can add that before we planned our Middle East tour, Senator Specter came to me and urged that Iraq be among the countries covered in our tour. We, therefore, consider this meeting important. We did not come to you with preconceptions or certain impressions. If Your Excellency agrees, the other congressmen may want to add something, or you may want to speak.

The president: Yes, I will speak about this. I am pleased you said you came without preconceptions that might prevent us from interacting with the facts as they really are. This is suitable not only for us, but also for humanity at large. We believe in a wise maxim that says: No matter what your size and strength, you should assume you are smaller and weaker than your adversary, so as to know him. It is only through this that you can enter the minds and hearts of people as they really are, not as you suppose or wish them to be. Against the backdrop of this wise maxim, I understand your statement that you came here without preconceptions.

In today's world, there are the big and the small, and we in reality know that the criterion is material capability. But we will not submit to this conception. We seek a criterion linked to the concepts of God almighty, who is greater than anything else. So, those who believe in fair play are the big; those who touch the fact as it is, not as they wish it to be, are the big; those who achieve or help achieve peace — not only for themselves, but also for humanity at large — are the big. And those who search for the truth in the case of a dispute between two or more parties are the big. Proceeding from these conceptions, I am glad to meet you in Iraq, and in one of the Iraqi cities whose civilization dates back more than 4,000 years. But one should not feel satisfied with talking only about history. One should seek to use history in the service of humanity. We are determined in this country to act — in order to feel good — not based only on national considerations, but also human considerations, whether concerning our region or remote areas on earth. It is true, we know, that we are a small country. We also know humanity needs both the big and the small. When an old man leaves the world, a young man moves along the road. The big cannot measure their size unless there are small ones around. So, even by material standards, a big one needs a small one to know he is big. On the other hand, the small is to be blamed, because if he were not small, the big would not grow big.

I thank you for this frankness in your letter, and I consider this frankness a key to a future based on sufficient clarity. Some may think frankness upsets Iraq when it is practiced in the Western democracies. But I say frankness does not upset us because it serves us in at least two areas: It guides us when we make mistakes, and it guides us when we do things right. We hold fast to the right when we find that the opposite frankness is unable to convince us of the contrary. We reconsider our policies and positions when we find that frankness showed up our mistakes and shook our convictions. I strongly believe this is the biggest result of exercising democratic rights.

I believe the Iraqi and American politicians need to know each other. They need to know the history of the two countries as to the basic factors related to social, cultural, and political life, because this knowledge is indispensable if one wants to draw the proper conclusions.

Therefore, as you are worried because of reports reaching you from Iraq and because of the policies you criticize, we also are worried because of reports we receive from the United States and about the policies you follow. Some Westerners sometimes confuse things. They imagine that when the Arabs speak of the Arab nation, they seek leadership for the Arab nation. And although, from the humanitarian and democratic viewpoints, we do not think this door should be closed, we would like to point out we believe that, being one nation, any weak Arab policy will reflect negatively on other Arab states. We have many examples. When Egypt weakens, Riyadh, Baghdad, and Amman become weak. When Riyadh becomes strong, this will reflect positively on Baghdad, Marrakesh, and Algiers.

Such a situation does not exist, for instance, in Western Europe, because Europe is composed of states and nations. The Arabs are composed of states, but they are one nation and one Arab mind affects another Arab mind, not only because they speak the same language, but because they have the same soul. They imbibe their culture from the same source. You therefore might find that there are various policies in the Arab homeland. Iraq has a policy, Saudi Arabia has a policy, Algeria has a policy, and Morocco has a policy. But when they are provoked, they all rise in the same direction. This should be taken into account, not in order to be destroyed and to be worked against, but to be understood with the aim of building firm bridges in ties between the Arab nation and the states and nations that seek good relations with the Arabs. Therefore, we are aware a large-scale campaign is being launched against us from the United States and Europe.

Senator Dole: Not from President Bush. Yesterday he told us he does not support this.

The president: You must have noticed we did not tell the Arabs to launch a countercampaign. Nevertheless, we find here in the Arab world a campaign is mounting against your policy toward us. Why is that? Before we ask this question, we ask: Are you not democratic in the United States? Do you not want peoples to exercise their democratic rights, something which is openly claimed in the United States? Do you not respect people's freedom? I know this is what the United States declares.

Senator Dole: It is [a] basic issue for us.

The president: Then does this not prompt you to reconsider your policies and ideas when you know an entire nation considers that the US, Israeli, and British attitudes imply a provocation to the entire nation and are unfair to Iraq? You know as well as I do that the Western media are more powerful than the Arab media. Therefore, the Western media were supposed to have convinced the Arab public of their logic and intentions within this period during which the campaign was launched. If the Western media failed to convince the Arab citizen of their logic, then there must be an error; this error is not a technical one, but is within the concept of truth and falsehood. Iraqi radio does not reach all parts of the Arab homeland, and you are aware that, technically and otherwise, the Third World countries have not reached superpower or big power capability.

According to these meanings, then, and in line with democratic concepts, I say the Arab nation considers the position against Iraq unfair and premeditated. I will discuss this issue again with the US Senate members, led by Mr. Dole. When I talk about excuses, I do not mean, for instance, to convince you of each excuse, because I know you differ completely with me on this issue. I do this only out of respect for you, and to make available for you some vocabulary to use with the officials in the United States so your excuses will be supported by something you have heard from the highest authorities in Iraq.

It is said Iraq has threatened Israel, although the speech is clear and is translated into English. The speech says, in the light of perception and conviction, that this campaign is intended to create the psychological, media, and political cover for Israel to attack us the way it did in 1981. The campaign also is similar to that which took place in 1981, though this one is harsher.

Senator Dole: Once more, I want to assert the US Government is not the cause of the campaign.

The president: Anyway, it is a campaign taking place in the United States.

Senator Dole: Mr. President, we condemned the Israeli attack in 1981.

The president: Yes, you condemned it. However, many reports showed the United States knew about it in advance.

Senator Dole: I am sorry I interrupted. I will talk about this later.

The president: If the United States did not know about the attack, the problem, then, is much bigger, because the United States is the one who is providing Israel with the elements of strength. So, if any superpower makes available the elements of strength to any country in the region or outside the region and cannot, to any extent, control the way it uses that strength, this is, then, what threatens peace. This, moreover, puts the world face to face with surprises whose results the world does not know how to control.

I come back to my statement. I said: If Israel strikes, we will strike back. I repeat now, in your presence, that if Israel strikes, we will strike back. I believe this is a fair stand. A stand known in advance is what helps peace, and not otherwise. For if Israel realizes it will be struck, it might refrain from striking. Then, if the West truly wants peace, such behavior is for the sake of peace. This behavior, furthermore, only disturbs those who want Israel to strike at Iraq without Iraq retaliating. I also have said: If Israel uses atomic bombs, we will strike at it with the binary chemical weapon. I reiterate now that if Israel does this, we will do that. We have given instructions to the commanders of the air bases and the missile formations that once they hear Israel has hit any place in Iraq with the atomic bomb, they will load the chemical weapon with as much as will reach Israel and direct it at its territory. For we might be in Baghdad holding a meeting with the command when the atomic bomb falls on us. So, to make the military order clear to the air and missile bases' commanders, we have told them if they do not receive an order from a higher authority, and a city is struck by an atomic bomb, they will point toward Israel any weapons capable of reaching it.

Mr. Dole, Senate members, I know chemical weapons were prohibited by the Geneva Convention. I know and I do not forget our commitments, nor the fact we signed it. But are chemical weapons more dangerous for humanity than nuclear bombs?

You are citizens and officials of a superpower. You know, scientifically and practically, the effect of each weapon. You also know that when chemical weapons were prohibited, this was an across-the-board prohibition. So, how can you ask Iraq not to use chemical weapons against atomic bombs used by a belligerent party that is continuously threatening the Arab nation? Are the atomic weapons more destructive than the hydrogenic?

Senator Dole: The hydrogenic are.

The president: Suppose that years before, a war broke out between you and the Soviet Union — because now an environment of detente is prevalent, thanks be to God, and this is good for humanity at large — and the Soviet Union used the atomic bomb against you. Will you be able to distinguish, when you strike back, the hydrogenic from the atomic? Then, how would it be if the opposite happened and the Soviet Union used the hydrogenic bomb? In this case, would you not use the atomic bomb?

Then, regardless of how the speech was interpreted by the media, the speech is as follows: If Israel strikes, we will strike at it. Our speech is clear. It is written in Arabic and English, and recorded on audio and video. We do not go back on what we say. If Israel strikes and uses atomic weapons, then we will use the binary chemicals. This is our stand, and it will not change. As to what some like to say about Iraq making threats, we do not apologize for the statement we made, because it is clear, just, and defensive, as well as a right. I also know the difference between possessing weapons and using them. I believe it is the Arabs' right to possess any weapon their enemy possesses. Iraq does not have the atomic bomb. If Iraq possessed it, we would declare so in order to maintain peace and to prevent Israel from using the atomic bomb. But, if any Arab state declares, now or a month later, that it possesses the atomic bomb, myself and the Iraqis will be the first to express support and respect for this action. Why? Don't I know the meaning of wars and their atrocities! Are we seeking wars and tragedies? We want peace. However, since we know the laws of the age, we realize peace cannot be achieved between an entity supported by all the modern forces of a superpower and an Arab entity that is still beginning the road. We do not want atomic, chemical, and biological weapons to spread. If the West truly wants the same thing, then let it declare the entire region must be clear of atomic, chemical, and biological weapons.

Who made the Arabs search for and produce chemical weapons? It was Israel. The Arabs know Israel has chemical, biological, and nuclear weapons. So, what do you expect the Arabs to do? Give up their homelands and abandon their peoples? Why is it assumed only Israel acts in a responsible manner when it comes to weapons, while Arabs do not? From a scientific viewpoint, hitting the Iraqi nuclear reactor amounts to a nuclear explosion. Some scientists believe there may be complications that may lead to contamination similar to that caused by the use of nuclear weapons. Israel hit the Iraqi nuclear reactor, which was on the outskirts of Baghdad.

The West denounces Iraq's possession of rocket systems and harasses Iraq for transferring technology and innovations regarding this. The West also is worried about the launch of the al-'Abid rocket, which has the capability of carrying satellites. However, it congratulates Israel when it launches a rocket or actually places a satellite in orbit.

Arabs hear affronts and insults directed against them by the West every day. Why? Has the control of the Zionist trend over you reached the extent that it deprives you of your humanity? Has patriotism in those countries become so weak that they no longer are able to say what is right and what is wrong? Is this the price for the electoral campaigns and the influence of the Zionist lobby on the outcome of those elections? If this is the case, then we — not trying to boast about anything, but to express our responsibility — believe Arabs now have an extra task, not only to liberate themselves, but also to liberate certain dark corners in the world from the extortion of the Zionist lobby. This only can be achieved through peace and only when Arabs prove a match for Israel. Then, we not only will be helping to liberate ourselves, but to liberate others from the weight of the Zionist pressure they are subjected to in the West.

We want peace. However, we do not want the price of peace to be the Arabs' submission and humiliation, or the usurpation of their land and rights. We want the peace that will put everyone on the same human level and give everyone the same human value, a peace in which the intent of the UN Charter is implemented.

We do not have the desire or intention of attacking anyone. We must say, however, that we have the determination and the willpower to retaliate against any aggression. Without having any intention other than to respect the human laws that exist in this age, we want to establish good relations with the United States, provided we feel certain the United States of America feels the same way.

I hope you will not be offended by my frankness, because I want to say something. You have said some members of Congress may ask for sanctions against Iraq. But, have you asked yourselves how you can impose sanctions against Iraq? You have not armed Iraq. You have not given it economic or financial aid. Instead, you carried out a witch- hunt against the Iraqis when they bought small technological items from the US market. You have neither brought us to power, nor do you protect us. You give missiles to Israel. And, when we possess a missile so we can tell Israel we have such and such a missile, you give Israel a missile to intercept our missile.

We do not consider this as directed against the security of Iraq alone, but also against the security of the Arabs. It also is an unjust position. A just peace is possible when, if Israel possesses one missile, the Arabs possess one missile, so neither can use it. Why, then, do you put pressure on or punish Iraq? You only punish Iraq when you engage in an act of aggression against it. Do you want to do this? We do not want to engage in any aggression against you; this is not our policy. But we are determined to resist anyone who engages in aggression against us. We will not be happy to have something happen, even if we are victorious. We are not happy war broke out between us and Iran, even though we emerged victorious, as you know. Had the Iranians been victorious, they would, perhaps, have been happy.

You know our real power lies in peace. We do not have any problem, nor are we unable to deal with the rules of the age creatively to thus escape wars and problems. But the people of the country that fought for eight years and sacrificed tens of thousands of their best men to protect the country's dignity cannot possibly avoid defending their pride, security, or sovereignty when they are threatened. When the people in your country hold opposite views to those of the leaders, only the president and a number of his administration officials fall. In our countries, on the other hand, when the people change their view of their leaders, the entire system falls; indeed the entire historical opportunity for development will collapse. The leaders of the Third World, therefore, care much about public opinion in their countries. Let us talk about ourselves. In Iraq, we have a high level of concern about Iraqi public opinion. Therefore, as you may have noticed, I used the same phrases used by Bush in my statement responding to his letter. If I fail to do this, I will personally look for someone else to lead the Iraqis — someone who can do it. If I do not do it, it means I do not respect Iraqi public opinion and dignity, or the equal rights of the Iraqis. In addition to this, you know we developed the missiles so they could reach Tehran after we had been hit for three years by Tehran's missiles.

I did not hear the West showing similar solidarity against the Iranian missiles when they hit Baghdad. I suggest you look back to this period or ask someone to do this for you. You will find that when we hit Tehran, the West termed this as escalation of the situation, although we warned Tehran and told the Iranians we possessed a missile that could hit Tehran to avert the possibility the Iranians would continue their attacks on Baghdad. But they thought we were not being truthful. After they repeated their attacks on Baghdad, we retaliated. In the battles of liberation, we did not use this missile against Tehran, although our superiority was known. We then thought about chemical weapons when Iran attacked us in al-Muhammara (Khurramshahr) with chemical weapons. These facts were documented by the military during the war, but we did not announce them. It is I who prevented their announcement at the time because the weapons were new and I feared it might create panic within the armed forces. This took place in al-Muhammara in 1980.

You are welcome. I have concluded my statement. If you do not feel tired, we will take a helicopter together and show you the map of Iraq so you can see its cities. We then will visit any city you admire, especially the Kurdish cities, so you can hear public opinion for yourselves. You can then convey what you see to your colleagues in Congress and the US Administration and whether you believe these people are persecuted or that Saddam Husayn kills the Iraqis, especially the Kurds, as alleged by the Western media and some Western politicicans.

We would like you to see the Iraqi people, if you feel you would like to.

Senator Robert Dole: I will discuss this with my colleagues. If there is enough time, I have a couple of remarks to make. There are basic differences between our two countries. We have a free media in the United States. When Your Excellency pronounces the word Western, I do not know if you mean the government. There was one person who was not authorized to say anything about the government. He was a commentator for VOA, which represents only the government. That person was fired. Please let me tell you only 12 hours ago, President Bush declared to me he wants better relations and that the US Government wants better relations with Iraq.

Your Excellency the President, we might better understand if we saw people. We believe, as leaders in the US Congress, that Congress does not represent Bush or the government. I assume Bush will object to the sanctions. He may veto them, unless something provocative occurs.

The US ambassador: As an American ambassador, I can confirm this is the US Government policy.

Senator Dole: We in Congress also try to exert our utmost efforts in this direction. The president may disagree with Congress. If he has a different viewpoint, he has the right to express it and exercise his powers. Your Excellency the President, I would like to say we know the importance of Iraq. You are the second country in oil reserves, your country is the second largest country in the region, and you have a deep-rooted history. We also understand Iraq's importance even in the peace process, although you are not the main party. When we talk about peace in the region, we mean peace for all countries in the region.

Regarding weapons, whether biological, chemical, or nuclear, we hope this will be part of a comprehensive settlement to make this region free of these kinds of weapons.

The president: That is fine by the Arabs.

Senator Dole: I would like to ask: How can we improve our relations when we read a report like this one: US television said yesterday that in the Salman Pak area south of Baghdad, you are developing a virus to destroy whole cities. This leaves a negative impression. Are you developing this virus, these germ weapons?

The president: Let us ask: Do the Americans not have biological weapons? Does Israel not have biological weapons? Does the world not have biological weapons, regardless of their use? Does the world not conduct research in this field, apart from weaponry?

Senator Dole: Not in the United States. Biological weapons have been renounced in the United States since the Nixon Administration.

The president: Is not research being done on them?

Delegation member: We conduct research, but there is no production of this type.

The president: Is not Cairo banned from conducting research in the biological field?

Senator Dole: Biological science is not banned, but the production of biological weapons constitutes a serious threat.

The president: I would like to explain to their excellencies, the Congress members, and say the following: We are aware of what the biological weapons mean. We are aware if such a method were used, the situation would become uncontrollable. Therefore, rest assured on this point. We speak about what we have. We also speak about what we will use if an aggression is mounted against us. Therefore, regardless of what is said in the papers, if we had biological weapons, we would have admitted it. If there is anyone in the world, if he is our enemy and fears biological weapons, let him come, and together we will scrap biological weapons.

Thus, we have no biological weapons, but we do have chemical weapons. But can President Bush tell me or tell the Iraqi National Assembly, as I have just told you about Iraq, that Israel has no biological weapons? I have spoken about what Iraq has, but can President Bush speak about Israel and say it has no biological weapons?

Senator McClure: We will ask him. We have no information, but we will ask him.

The president: Then let us agree. I have said Iraq has no biological weapons, because Iraq is aware of the danger of toying with this issue.

As to whether scientists have done research on this or that sort of germ, I do not give a guarantee in this matter, and I do not deny it. Therefore, let us agree. Chemical, biological, and nuclear weapons are a threat to the world, and it is our duty to cleanse the world, one region after another, of these weapons. Here I speak of Iraq. Therefore, it is certain there are nuclear and chemical weapons in our region. If we search carefully, we might discover biological weapons. It is in the interest of the world, and in the interest of peace and security in the region and the world to cleanse this region and to establish an accurate, true and fair system of inspection. Then and only then will we be fair in our methods.

Senator Dole: Mr. President, I would like to ask only one thing. I highly welcome what you have said, that this policy is the definite government policy. But how can we implement what you have said? This is another question. But I think we will try to do so. The point I want to make is that I can appreciate your feelings about the importance of providing means of defense for yourselves. However, the world is viewing the development of mass destruction weapons with the feeling they mean an increased threat to mankind.

The president: This is true, and we have the same feelings. Moreover, we do not want these weapons to exist in the region.

Senator Dole: I do not know everything the US Government knows, but I do not know that there is a biological capability in the Israeli arsenal. I also would like to make a simple distinction for us to understand each other. There is a difference between basic scientific research and attempts to develop biological weapons.

The president: I mean conventional scientific research, not germ warfare. I mean using germs for scientific purposes. I am aware that conducting research on germs for military purposes amounts to using them as a weapon.

Tariq 'Aziz: You must have heard President Saddam Husayn state he is prepared to declare the entire Middle East a free zone.

The president: Including Iran.

Tariq 'Aziz: Yes, including Iran and the whole region — to be declared free of all types of weapons of wholesale destruction. It is an official statement binding on the Iraqi Government, and you may repeat it. You are going to Israel. Can you get the Israeli Government to issue a comparable declaration?

You are knowledgeable about Israel's policies, Senator. I do not think you can secure a commitment from the Israeli prime minister as clear as the one made by President Saddam Husayn.

Senator Dole: If you will allow me, as a member of the delegation, I will work toward getting such a declaration.

Tariq 'Aziz: You had sought such a declaration from the president of Iraq, and you got it. I see you will likewise seek a comparable statement from the Israelis, and you will not get it. I hope you will say as much in Congress.

Senator Dole: If an opportunity should present itself, I will ask for the same assurance from Iranian leaders, except I am denied even the chance of saying hello or talking to them.

The president: But we ought to promote the notion. I think the idea would prove favorable to the world and the region. It may be that the time is right to float such a proposal in Israel.

Instead of thinking of applying sanctions against Iraq, Congress ought to be contemplating sanctions against Israel if it fails to respond to such ideas.

Senator Murkowski: I believe, Mr. President, that we came to your country aware of Middle East history, accepting there has been a conflict in the region, that you still are in conflict with Iran after a long war, and that you are still reordering things in your country. In the United States I think we see the Middle East as a volatile tinderbox where there are huge stockpiles of arms and advanced technological weapons. In Eastern Europe we now have a climate of peace.

When we look at this part of the world, we find tension is very high. We have come to see you, Mr. President, in good faith. We are looking forward to the chances that present themselves. An attempt now is being made in Israel to form a new government. It seems to me there is a golden opportunity now. In our discussions with all heads of state in the region, they expressed their firm conviction there is a favorable opportunity. But for real peace to be attained, there must be a commitment on all sides to reach a compromise, as happens in our legislative bodies in the United States. That is, we have to agree on a compromise. I think the message we are bringing you, Mr. President — a message from the president of the United States — is to urge you, as leader of this country, to join other leaders in the region to make the most of this opportunity. I highly appreciate your frankness and views regarding the defense of your country and this is something we understand and feel that there is a similar concern in Israel, as they realize there exists a chance which they have to use.

The president: To date, this does not seem to be the case.

Senator Murkowski: I understand this.

The president: This is because one cannot be convinced that he who embarks on a broad immigration to the occupied territories really wants peace. Where would he settle this number of immigrants? You know Gaza has a very high population density. You know this also is the case with Jerusalem and the other occupied territories. They can hardly absorb a very small number of people.

We view the number of immigrants and this immigration as the basis for new expansion.

Senator Howard Metzenbaum: There are large areas in the Negev to absorb the immigrants.

The president: If the Negev were suitable to live in, those who are now in Israel would have settled there.

Senator Metzenbaum: Some people are building settlements in the Negev.

The president: It is only a limited number of people.

Senator Alan Simpson: I enjoy meeting with frank and direct people. It is difficult for us in the wild West — the cowboys — to understand that when we lose a case sometimes, we do not lose our life. This was one of the reasons that made the five of us — who are, as Senator Dole has said, leaders in the Senate — call the president yesterday. We told the president our visit to Iraq will cost us dearly, as it will make us lose popularity and so many people will attack us for visiting Iraq. Senator Metzenbaum has showed great courage by coming with us at this moment. President Bush told us, however: Go. I want you to go. There are so many topics that we must raise with the Iraqis. Some of those topics have been raised by Senator Dole, and they also are included in the message. I read to President Bush the message we wrote to Your Excellency. President Bush had at his side his assistant for national security affairs, Scowcroft.

There is something that has to be said after all that. There is no conspiracy by the US Government, or in England or Israel, to attack this country. The other thing is that the president said: If you are criticized for visiting Iraq, I will defend and speak out for you. The things that you said and talked about now, however, are the same things we in the United States of America have said about the Soviet Union — who will strike first? Who will press the button first? Who will turn half of the United States into a fireball? In the process, and we say this now, we spent large sums of money. Now we are going to reduce our military budget by about $150 to $180 billion, whether the peace efforts or talks go on or not.

I would like you to know, Mr. President, that Secretary of State Baker and Foreign Minister Shevardnadze have become friends, and they go fishing together, and that Field Marshal Akhromeyev and Crowe, chairman of the U.S. Joint Chiefs of Staff, have now begun to set up a peace organization.

The president: This is because both of you want peace and have the will for it.

Tariq 'Aziz: There is no Gorbachev in Israel.

Senator Alan Simpson: One may emerge.

The president: If there were a wise man in Israel, he would have done the impossible to achieve peace now, not 10 years from now.

Senator Simpson: We all realize they must adopt a different position in the government. I say, however, that Presidents Bush and Gorbachev now are getting closer to each other, and they now have a personal relationship. Finally, you talk about democracy. Democracy is a very irksome and confusing thing. I believe your problem is with the Western media, not with the US Government, because you are isolated from the media and the press. The press is spoiled and conceited. All the journalists consider themselves brilliant political scientists. They do not want to see anything succeeding or achieving its objectives. My advice is that you allow those bastards to come here and see things for themselves.

The president: They are welcome. We want them to come and see, and then let them write freely. Let them, for instance, say: We like this and we don't like that. We do not have ill feelings toward them at all. I wish the media men would come. I authorize the ambassador to give a positive reply to all the reporters of the United States. We welcome whoever wants to come here: there is no veto on anyone. However, if you please, I would like to make a comment.

Delegation member: They will go after me when I get back.

The president: If you please, I have a remark to make. I realize the media sometimes are a nuisance, even for the politics of a country. Three days ago I was reading the local papers. I read a complaint by a woman from al-Qadisiyya Governorate against officials there. The woman says a citizen demolished her home with a shovel, so she lodged a complaint with the competent authorities. There was no response to her complaint. The time was 0815. I telephoned al-Qadisiyya governor, read him the complaint, and told him to immediately go in his car to the place and meet with the lady and the officials in charge there, and then to call me back, no matter where I was, after he had found out the facts. He called me before noon the same day and told me what happened was that while the lady was building, she encroached upon the adjacent land, which belongs to the citizen she is talking about, and that the citizen has lodged a complaint with the Iraqi judiciary and won his suit to eliminate the building from his land. The role of the executive authorities in this case was that they had implemented the judiciary's decision. Then the governor asked me: What are your orders? I answered: I do not order anything. This is his right. However, I wanted then to call the editor in chief of the newspaper that published the complaint and tell him he should have confirmed the truth of the complaint before publishing it. I did not call, however. Because had I called, the editor in chief might have thought Saddam Husayn, who advocates freedom of the press, was interfering with something that could limit freedom of publicaton.

I go back to the media campaign and wonder, along with you gentlemen: If governments are not responsible for disseminating what happens — or, let us say if the US Government is not responsible for propagating what happened, how then, was this huge amount produced in such a short time?

Senator Alan Simpson: It is very simple.

The president: Then, there has to be a party behind all this.

Senator Alan Simpson: They feed on each other. Each one of them eats part of the other. A front-page report in *Newsweek* is taken by another reporter and published by him in turn.

The president: Let us review the matter of the capacitors, for example. If they were prohibited, it was enough to tell whoever wanted to buy them that they did not sell them. If they were prohibited in Iraq only, why did US intelligence get involved in such a complex arrangement? First, selling the capacitors, then agreeing with British intelligence that as soon as the cargo arrived at London airport, it should be seized and then shown on television? This is, of course, a government, not a media, action. Moreover, consider what happened to the Iraqi employee who was expelled. Up to this time when I am talking to you, and I am telling the truth, the only thing I know is that we have an employee in New York who is carrying out his duties according to US law. And all of a sudden we were told: You have to call your employee back. Who in my country would task this employee with an illegal action? The first thing that came to my mind was to ask the intelligence service. They have given a formal reply and told me, and the Foreign Ministry as well, that this is neither in our plans, nor is it our policy, and that they have not contacted this man from far or near or assigned him any task. We do not have an objective of this kind in the whole United States.

Tariq 'Aziz: I am sure our position is sound, and I explained to Senator Dole that the person accused of attempted murder is a cook and a simple man with a family, that his children and wife live in the United States, and that he cannot be a criminal.

The president: If he had intended to kill, at least he would have sent his family back.

Senator James McClure: I and Senator Metzenbaum are members of the Congressional Security Committee (as heard) and we will investigate this matter carefully.

The president: My second and last remark about the media is that if the media in my country harm our relations with a country with which we want to establish good relations, and I cannot intervene to prevent it, I will go on television, go to the radio station, and write in newspapers to tell the truth and declare my view to correct the press.

Senator Howard Metzenbaum: Your Excellency the President, you already know that I am a Jew and that I vigorously support Israel. I had some reservations about my visit.

The president: I am sure you will not be sorry.

Senator Metzenbaum: I am not sorry. Your Excellency the President, you are portrayed in the Western media in a very negative way. I am not the right person to be your pubic relations man. But let me propose something, as I am interested in peace more than any other specific factor. I do not want to talk about giving up the West Bank, half of Jerusalem, or any other part. This issue is up to the parties concerned. After listening to you for about an hour, I realized you are strong and an intelligent man, and that you want peace. But I also believe you are concerned over what has happened in the past in connection with the United States, Israel, or anyone else. If a certain shift in your thinking makes you concentrate on the peace we need in the Middle East, there will be no other leader in the Middle East who can be compared with you. Your Excellency the President, if you stress this point, I believe your excellency can be a very effective force for peace in the Middle East. As I said, I am not your public relations man.

Senator Dole: I am described in the United States as stubborn. President Bush wanted to build a warmer and more sympathetic America, and I wanted a stronger America.

The president, jesting: In this issue, we tend to go with President Bush.

Senator Dole: There is something I would like to say, since you have invited reporters to come here. Why don't you ask them to go to the place where they claim biological weapons are produced? Challenge them to prove that you speak nothing but the truth.

The president: I assure you we will lose nothing if we ask them where the biological weapons are and also ask them to lead us to them. But we know these media organs as you do. They are like a spoiled child. If this child is given a sweet in response to his desires and cries, he will continue to cry all the time.

Senator Dole: The media have a role to play, and I do not think the media are wrong all the time.

The president: Neither are they always right.

Senator Dole: I always say they are wrong all the time, especially given that they attack me. I am not talking about myself, Mr. President, as I hesitate to do that. Because I lost my right arm in action 40 years ago, I am being daily reminded that all of us have to work, since all of us have our differences. We sometimes despise each other for certain reasons or in the context of certain issues. I, therefore, would like to emphasize to you before we leave Iraq that this is a very important visit. As King Husayn told us, there exists a window of opportunity that we must make sure not to let pass. Maybe it will take another war, another decade, or 30 years before another such opportunity comes along. This leads me to the last point that I want to make. We have to work for our bilateral relations. If there is anything we can do to improve our ties, it will be beneficial to both our nations if we do. If there is a message you would like us to relay for you to President Bush, we would gladly pass it on, as we are going to meet with him upon our return to report to him on this auspicious visit.

The president: Give him my compliments and an account of our meeting. Tell him Iraq reciprocates his desire to improve ties for us to consolidate a relationship based on mutual respect and interests, as well as advancing the cause of peace and security globally and in our region. I am glad we have met and talked openly. I would like to tell you something, incidentally. When, for instance, *The New York Times* says something slighting about Iraq, it is reported by many radio stations, not only in the United States, but in the West as a whole. It will not do for Baghdad's *al-Jumhuriyya* to refute *The New York Times,* as no one will read it. In this case, the job falls to the Iraqi foreign minister, the undersecretary at the Foreign Ministry, or sometimes Saddam Husayn for us to be heard, because we have no chance otherwise. We may be criticized for this. For example, a newspaper or 10 newspapers may launch a campaign which the information minister will have to address. Besides, we are entitled to be skeptical, having been bitten more than once. Over time, and on the strength of good will generated by actual behavior, our ties will be fostered and the groundwork will be laid for clear relations, and thus the future will be free from major obstacles. I am not saying the future will be trouble-free, since it is in the nature of things that there should be differing viewpoints and divergent policies.

Senator Dole: Even within families.

Senator Simpson: I practiced law in a small town for 18 years, during which 1,500 divorce cases came my way. All I did was listen to people, and all that they wanted was for someone to listen to them. Every divorce case was brought on because of the coldness of the partners. In other words, there was a breakdown of communication. Self-righteousness, pride, and opinionatedness led to separation. It is highly important, Mr. President, that even while we argue and yell at each other and fight each other we must still keep up rather than discontinue the dialogue. Otherwise, the world will be shaken by an enormous divorce.

I am not a peaceful person; I like argument and struggle. A while back, President Bush said he hates broccoli, since his mother used to force it on him, and that is why he decided never to eat it. American media have written extensively on this anecdote. Some newspaper articles argued that President Bush, after all, is not the wimp he was made out to be. We, therefore have to (sentence incomplete as heard)...

The president: I understand the import of your words, which fit the entire gamut of international relations, with the following exception:

If a president from the smallest African state visits me, you will see me driving his car, playing host to him, and doing things outside protocol. However, if a president of a big power visits me, I will not do for him anything outside the protocol. There is an equality between my country and the African's. He will not misunderstand me when I deal with him outside protocol. However, Gorbachev might misunderstand my behavior to the detriment of our relations. I do not want our relations to be harmed.

Therefore, the United States, at least within the foreseeable future, should either enter people's minds and hearts, or lose all the people on this globe. Both probabilities are on the same level, for reasons of which you are aware. Therefore, the United States is required to show wisdom in dealing with small states more than the small states are required to show wisdom in dealing with it. The United States is required to bear more than the small and medium-sized states can, because no one will say America is weak and cannot bear up, that its president is weak, that its economic resources are weak, that its political resources are ineffective. They will say the United States behaves wisely and responsibly. Then the United States will be more effective, and the benefits it will reap this way will be more than the benefits it reaps the other way. You are welcome.

Senator James McClure: I believe that over the past four days, we have had the honor of meeting with heads of state. We have had the opportunity of talking openly with you. We are all committed to conveying these things when we go to Israel under Senator Dole's leadership. We have fairly reached the conclusion that an opportunity exists for a peaceful solution and a settlement of the Middle East problem, that the realization of this settlement is possible, and that your assurances today and your desire increase our commitment to conveying these things to Israel and to conveying the feeling that this opportunity exists now, because very few Americans and very few Israelis have had the opportunity that we have had.

The president: You are, of course, free to voice your convictions. However, I hope you will not forget that for us, the Arabs, those who represent the Palestinian issue are the Palestinians, led by Yasir 'Arafat. I believe it is now clear that anyone who tries to deal with the Palestinian issue on behalf of the Palestinians without being entrusted with such a task will fail to reach a peaceful solution. And because we want a just solution, because we want peace, we had better enter houses through their doors. The doors of this issue are the Palestinians.

Senator: Thank you.

The president: I am very pleased. I wish you success.

Source: FBIS-NES-90-074, 17 April 1990.

4. Saddam Husayn Addresses Arab Summit 28 May 1990

Speech by Iraqi President Saddam Husayn at the opening of the extraordinary Arab summit in Baghdad on 28 May 1990 — live. *Baghdad Domestic Service in Arabic 1039 GMT, 28 May 1990.*

In the name of God, the merciful, the compassionate. Ye are the best of peoples, evolved for mankind, enjoining what is right, forbidding what is wrong, and believing in God (Koranic verse).

Esteemed, brothers, brother leaders of Arab states, Your Majesties, Excellencies, and Highnesses, peace be upon you, and you are welcome in Baghdad. You know how glad and proud this city is in your coming together, and how welcoming of you it is. In addition to the implications of this gathering in this city, Baghdad recalls its historical significance, and remembers its role and responsibilities in the present circumstances, being the city which the Arabs founded when they carried the torch of light to all humanity to convey the divine message that God honored them to spread once they believed in it. It is the city that has kept the faith, as you have known it, with its history and the lofty meanings that accompanied its growth in the era of Abu-Ja'far al-Mansur.

Brothers, you are in your country, Iraq. Every citizen would like us to express ourselves on his behalf and be guided both in word and deed by that which is befitting to the status of this occasion when we welcome you and facilitate your stay and your work — which all Arabs hope will be glorious and successful. You are welcome, brothers and esteemed audience.

Brothers, a few days ago, specifically on 22 May, a new dawn arose in Yemen when it became one Yemen — one country, and one leadership, as it was in the days when it flourished and was a rich fountain of Arabism and Arab civilization. Here it is today, deservedly inheriting that eternal heritage led by brother President 'Ali 'Abdallah Salih, with his brother deputy 'Ali Salim al-Bayd at his side. May they be blessed with this major and historical accomplishment. May the Yemeni people be blessed in their unity. And may all the leaders of Yemen be blessed with the truthfulness of their call that accompanied their unity. May all Yemen's faithful leaders and people be blessed with this determined will and selflessness, after they weathered bitterness in divisionism, so that they may reap all the benefits of the unity of Yemen. May all the Arabs be blessed by this dawn in the sky of Arabism.

Brothers, we are meeting in Baghdad to work together to realize whatever God may guide us to do under a keynote set for the conference, namely, pan-Arab security and threats to it, how to tackle them, and other related issues. During every conference which brings Arabs together on the summit level, children of the Arab nation everywhere await with eagerness and hope what it will produce, and pray to God that their leaders will measure up to their expectations. This conference, however, is being convened under special circumstances, and is therefore especially important. The current Arab and international circumstances add up to a unique factor that only a few of the previous summits share.

Since we believe, in accordance with our countries' laws, in the importance of the people and that they are the source of power, it is our constitutional and national duty to ensure that the topics of the summit, its decisions, and our behavior and thinking, must relate closely to what we know and sense about the mood of public opinion in the Arab community. We will thus be doing our peoples a special favor. Although the title of the conference, the events related to it, and its timing might indicate that the circumstances are transient and concerned only with the immediate present, we, nonetheless, think that laying solid foundations for concepts underlying these subjects, and the measures needed to put them into practice, extend into the future. We will shed an inextinguishable beam of light into that future that will, God willing, guide the nation toward working in an atmosphere without setbacks and where gaps are closed. This will take place after the Arabs have joined forces to extract the teeth of the ferocious wolves that have pounced on them to thwart their progress and destroy their hopes for a proud present and a better future, and will renew their nation's human role, which is always to try to attain every national and humanitarian objective.

Not every Arab man in the street may be aware of the headings, which have been formulated on modern principles, to be the agenda of our summit. Not every average Arab may be as aware as we who are assembled here are of the detailed and comprehensive implications of pan-Arab security and the requirements for its preservation, or how to express them in reassuring and effective words. But through a sense of history, the Arab masses know the correct answer to the question of how the Arabs can improve their lot. They are also aware that the Arabs are best served by avoiding greed, spite, intrigue, and by closing their ranks through thick and thin. The Arab masses also realize that their interests are best served by presenting a united front against aggression and by pooling their resources whenever the need arises, and making their deeds match their rhetoric.

As 21 states, we must present a solid front against whomever deviates from pan-Arab security within our ranks so that we can contain his whims and policies. Our positions, therefore, must be open so we can interact as leaders and so that the Arab masses can respond to what is correct among these policies and be prepared to take the proper action and make the required sacrifices. The Arab masses believe that pan-Arab security is an integral whole and that for pan-Arab security to become a reality, we cannot afford to regard it halfheartedly — it must be practiced in every aspect of life. It is not possible to divorce popular matters from official and material ones, or the information field from the military.

Brothers, we both know that a nation comprising 21 regimes — taking into consideration the circumstances, capabilities, and views unique to each regime — must have certain differences in viewing any issue or any situation. Because we are a single nation, however, duty demands that we concentrate on points of agreement and elements that connect the single nation, and that we depend on these.

The peculiar elements of uniqueness and nationalism — elements that are well known — do not merit our concentration or focus, nor do we need to call attention to them, because these elements in themselves — which are derived from everyday experience, and from things that are normal in our present circumstances — are able to attract attention to themselves, and to impose their weight at any time, without effort or endeavor.

We are not in a sufficient state of complete pan-Arab unity to call attention to the importance of national or local uniqueness, or to the interest groups within their own countries, taking into consideration different views, decisions, and policies. We are not talking about a constitution for unity to do so. Therefore, stressing pan-Arab action, its principles, and the policies it mandates, in addition to the serious sacrifice needed in this regard, is a kind of jihad in some of its aspects, because it is not a normal state of affairs, but a state of rising up to a new level of thought and action, and is something that should be asserted. We should also stress the elements of unity that merit consideration when we make a decision regarding the unified stance mandated by pan-Arab action and security.

Proceeding from the above, many elements must be considered: the great disparity in the level of economic development; in wealth; in cultural, scientific, and technical development; in addition to the levels of general capability and the way of expressing this capability — whether through accepting or rejecting foreign offers — and the way of dealing with the foreigners' illegitimate ambitions and policies, in addition to others. These elements might all create gaps in the wall of pan-Arab security, unless we know how to deal with these elements and circumstances and how to remedy their negative aspects. Some of the aforementioned elements might destroy national and pan-Arab relations, capabilities, and desires. They might also constitute an obstacle to these relations, preventing them from developing in the way they should. This is because the strength and weakness of what is national is related to pan-Arab weakness and strength, and because adding pan-Arab thought and conduct to what is national constitutes a basic goal and the correct ideological framework for what is national. Moreover, this will provide encouragement and inspiration for every manifestation of strength and capability of the national character within our countries. This alone can rid the sons of the nation of that feeling and dual conduct (both pan-Arab and national) that is imposed by the fact that we are — and this is not a fictitious statement — sons of a single nation, but at the same time we suffer from this state of national and local division, indulging ourselves in its narrow details and giving attention and concentration to it, to the extent of seeming, at times, to lack any readiness or ability to link national considerations with pan-Arab ones. Let us give what is pan-Arab and what is national, as we said earlier, the correct strength and capability. Let us move together, in all our countries, with steady, unfaltering steps to a new level of our mission and what is related to this mission — capabilities, plans, and endeavors. The danger of duality, bearing in mind the fact that we are a single nation and not many, and that this fact is not reflected in the general policies and their ramifications — foreign, internal, economic, social, cultural, and military — does not only lie in the psychological and ideological disturbance and disorder it creates. It also has an impact on the overall pattern of life in general and on the citizen's relationship with his nation, and the relationship of the ruler or leader with his people.

One of the causes of Arab weakness is the reluctance on the part of both peoples and their leaders to formulate or take a unified position that would guarantee their policy and its direction, and which would provide the moral strength and material momentum to reach our set targets. This escapes our minds sometimes even in your country, Iraq, in which you are now present.

If we want the resolutions of this summit to fulfill the hopes that our nation has pinned on us and which it expects from us, we must remember the feelings and views of our families in our homes over the past few weeks, the feelings and views of our personal friends among the people, and the feelings and views of those whom we have met from among the sons of our nation, including those who came to Baghdad to attend the Arab popular conference of the federations, trade unions, and professional and popular organizations, and its resolutions, and the stands taken by the press all over the Arab homeland. Then, when we respond — and we are determined to do so, God willing — and when we deal carefully with what the sons of our nation want, we will have found a position commensurate with our responsible view and in harmony with our pan-Arab, humanitarian standpoint.

Only by taking such a position can the leaders and their peoples be heading in the same direction. This is a great honor and I do not think that anyone of us will concede it. It is necessary to fulfill this wish and to add new strength and power to the Arab nation, in addition to the strength and resources in our respective countries.

Only then will we view pan-Arab security from a better perspective
than the narrow one considered by the traditionalists in the
technocratic bodies. These technocrats regard this security as a
technical matter, based on close links in terms of the personal
security, available information, state organizations, and their local
activity, to achieve only local aims, by preventing hostile forces
from penetrating it. Thus, they take a narrow view of matters. I say
we must rise to another view, proposing to tackle pan-Arab security
from a comprehensive viewpoint, both national and pan-Arab,
similar to our responsibility as strategists. Thus, we find this reflected
in the people's satisfaction with our general policies and in the
optimism for the future and the feeling of self-confidence. We find
the faithful people eager to safeguard our regimes and ready to
defend them. There is an inseparable connection between the regime,
its policies, its stands, and its capabilities, on the one hand, and the
Arab homeland and the entire nation and their capability, stability,
and prosperity, on the other, both during certain historical periods
and at all other times.

In a private meeting, one of the Arab figures from a fraternal
Arab country asked how and why the Iraqis had succeeded in
fighting all these many years until they triumphed — in the name of
the Arabs and in the name of God — and the darkness was defeated.
We discussed human aspects of the second al-Qadisiyya battle (with
Iran), which is your battle. Briefly, I say to you that whoever thinks
that the battle is only a technical matter is mistaken. He is mistaken
if he thinks that in terms of results and significance, the battle is
merely a military confrontation made necessary when one country
in the world is forced to wage such a confrontation. He is mistaken if
he thinks that it is a confrontation only between material resources,
and that the triumph will be based on weightier resources or superior
technology. It is much deeper and more extensive than this. In terms
of time and preparations, the confrontation is not confined to the
beginning of the armed struggle, and its results will not emerge in
accordance with what is wished. It extends much deeper than this. It
is a matter of life in all its ramifications, expertise in all fields, and
capabilities everywhere. It is related to conviction, rights, capabili-

ties, resolution, and creativity in both its moral and material aspects.

The essential factor in your experience in the second al-Qadisiyya, which is connected with actions and their outcome, is that we never promised the people anything unless we were convinced of it, and unless we were eager to realize it in the first place. And when we did promise, we always bound ourselves to our word of honor and to noble stands. We did not hesitate or procrastinate after having resolved to do something, but relied on God.

We always have viewed all areas and quarters of our country and all Arab areas and quarters — especially those good men who were prepared to support and back us — and all classes of our people as a pool of resources and capabilities that could be advanced forward and elevated upward. Thus, the future has come very near to — if not already united with — the present, and the past has become a living backdrop for the present in all its glory and significance. The past is basically connected with the practical and spiritual relationship between the responsibility of the position and its human aspects on the one hand, and between the human aspects of good citizenship and its responsibility on the other.

Taking into account one of your successful experiences in the life of Arabs in the contemporary era, fighting injustice and usurpation cannot be viewed within a traditional, technical perspective. The comparison in forces between ourselves and our enemies cannot be confined only to available resources. This comparison must be extended to the flood of resources that can be created by the historically correct position of the people and the nation, the faithful enthusiasm without which no guns will be able to realize any effective result, those resources that are connected with the tangible and the intangible, a comprehensive view of all life's requirements, and an optimistic view of the future and our self-confidence, while at the same time building on the foundation of our present resources.

When we rely on God — and we do rely on God — and depend on deep fraternal dialogue conducted in an atmosphere of strong interaction for better performance and encouraging brightness in our hearts; and when we recall — without ever forgetting — the standpoint of our nation, which we know very well; when we depend on our elements of strength, having analyzed them; when we locate, after careful study, the causes of our weakness and deal with them with common responsibility; when we fear nobody but God as we move toward unity; and when we depend on our peoples and nation, which have proved capable of shouldering their responsibility under extremely complicated circumstances — only then we can guarantee for ourselves a strength that knows no weakness, that does not abandon established rights, that can look confidently toward a better future, and that can restore every lost right — especially our right to dear Palestine, which is waiting impatiently to see Arab flags, especially the Palestinian flag, flying over it and over the domes of holy Jerusalem.

If the strongest and most powerful action within our nation is not sufficient to constitute the foundation for the nation's common action and policy, then the nation and the leaders of the Arab countries now meeting in Baghdad are advised to avoid the danger and mistake of constructing the nation's position and policies on the foundations of less capable or less well-prepared action, or on the weakest Arab position. If the policies of a group are built on the weakest or least efficient of its stances, then all steps thereafter will be based on a mistaken foundation and we will arrive too late — if the deadly monsters, so to speak, have not eaten up every member of the group, one after another, before the group arrives at its destination and goal. If this mistake occurs, the nation will suffer horrible setbacks, God forbid, and it will be deprived of energy and action — the last, most capable and efficient energy and action in the nation. In that event, we will lose many opportunities and increase the enemies' ambitions, rather than make the enemies reluctant and afraid to harm the nation, its security, and its sovereignty.

Those who are less capable among us must work hard for greater ability that matches, is integrated with, and interacts with what is agreed on by the group so that those in the lead can see and interact with those in the rear. And the whole group must encourage those with greater ability to move forward with all their support and good wishes of success, without letting this lead the more capable ones into adventurism or isolation.

We must regard the power of any Arab state as belonging to all, unless it is used against the Arab nation. By the same token, weakness in any one of our countries is bound to affect all of us, and it will constitute a crack in the wall of our pan-Arab security. Wherever weakness develops, it must respond to any offer of help from the more powerful Arab states in order to rid itself of its weakness, especially when weakness would undermine our stance *vis-à-vis* foreign powers, and could manifest itself in the granting of facilities to these foreign powers out of fear, thus compromising the Arab nation and its pan-Arab security. In the event of an Israeli attack, the Arabs must guard against a short-lived response. This is because Israeli force is based on the strategy of attacking major targets in the shortest period of time possible and with a minimum of losses to its military, economic, and manpower resources. And since the resources of the Arab nation cannot be quickly mobilized for reasons related to the spread of the Arab homeland, and given that we are 21 countries, among other reasons, it would not be possible for us to deploy our resources in the right places at short notice. Therefore, it behooves us to declare clearly that if Israel attacks and strikes, we will strike powerfully. If it uses weapons of mass destruction against our nation, we will use against it the weapons of mass destruction in our possession. There will be no concession on the liberation of Palestine. The United States has demonstrated that it is primarily responsible for the aggressive and expansionist policies of the Zionist entity against the Palestinian Arab people and the Arab nation — never mind the occasional disagreement it professes with this or that stance or behavior of the Zionist entity. It would not have been possible for the Zionist entity to engage in aggression and expansion at the Arabs' expense if it did not possess the force and political cover provided by the United States — the main source of the Zionist entity's aggressive military force, and the main source of its financial resources. It is the United States that largely provides the political cover for the Zionist entity's policies through Washington's intransigent stands at the UN

Security Council and its exercise of the veto to thwart condemnation of the Zionist aggressive policies and crimes.

Arab security and interests are on the receiving end of these American policies. We have to say as much to the United States without equivocation. We have to tell the United States that it cannot afford to pursue such policies and at the same time claim the friendship of the Arabs. This is not a policy of friendship. It is a harmful policy that threatens the security and vital interests of the Arab nation. If we say as much to the United States in unison and with the same tone and power and clarity, I am confident that Washington will take us and our interests seriously. Then, it will make its mind up one way or another. If the United States should then decide to be a friend to the Arabs, the Arabs would be happy, since then Washington will have based its friendship on reciprocity and mutual respect, and refrain from bringing harm to the Arabs. This is what the Arabs want.

The Arab nation must formulate its ties with other states on the basis of their stands on Arab rights, interests, and pan-Arab security.

Based on these facts, which were proven by tangible experience, no Israeli aggression against the Arab nation can be isolated from the desire of American imperialism in this regard. I use the word "imperialism" only here. In fact I have not used this word for a long time. But when I saw the memorandum presented by the groups working at the US State Department, indicating that we should not use the word imperialism, I decided to use it.

Based on these facts, which have been verified by tangible experience, no Israeli aggression against the Arab nation can be isolated from the designs and the support of US imperialism in this regard. This requires that we build a unified response to this aggression and against those who shield it and supply it with its requirements in all fields and domains. Then the nation will be in a better condition, and we will all be in better shape. The Arab nation will have the opportunity for serious, genuine, and deep relations with all world states, including the United States.

Only then will we be in a better condition and better position, and only then will we be more effective and more worthy of winning solid respect in the world. We must announce with a strong voice that no one, whoever he may be, can enjoy our resources and wealth at the same time that he is fighting us and opposing our scientific and technological progress. We must transform this principle into policy and words to be implemented and unanimously adhered to. Everyone must realize that success in battles with the enemies — when these battles become necessary — cannot be realized once the dust of footsteps and gun smoke begin covering their arenas. It begins with the preparations and solidarity in the social, economic, political, and information fields and with the successful preparations to realize aims in all walks of life and on both popular and official levels. This will be based on the principle that our fate is one, our future is in the same direction, aggression against any one of us is an aggression against all of us, and the enemy of any one of us is an enemy of the entire nation. Confronting this enemy will be comprehensive in terms of pooling the nation's resources in the same direction — territorial waters, airspace, territories, sea straits, canals — all of them will be placed in the service of the battlefronts and armies. Stands on these issues will be open and aboveboard. Then the Arab nation may not necessarily need military battles to safeguard all of its rights and regain the lost rights.

Brothers, at the Arab Cooperation Council summit held in Amman on 24 March 1990, we talked about international developments and our positions regarding them. Not much time has passed since then. We will make the analysis we presented in Amman a basis for a brotherly and thorough discussion, which will be enriched with your broad experience and with your awareness of, and viewpoints and information on, the turbulent international surroundings. Our deep-rooted nation, which has diverse and major resources, will be able to proudly stand fast in the face of the negative consequences resulting from the developments. It will also be able to interact with the positive consequences and deal with the new international surroundings in accordance with directions and formulas that are in harmony with its interests and obligations, which cannot be separated from the nation's security.

I would like to add something to the analysis I made in Amman:

The conflict between the two giants, the hateful division of the world in light of the influence and interests of these giants at that time, as well as the effect of their artillery shells which fell in the theater of conflict — which the arena of the Arab nation and community were not safe from — have severely harmed our nation and disturbed the balance of its character. Our nation, therefore, has not adopted a single, clear approach compatible with its heritage and independence and appropriate for its greatness. The forces of this nation — or, let us say, a major part of its forces — have been split between the influence of the two superpowers, their interests and strategies. This influence extends to popular and official quarters and positions. Our attention, thus, has been diverted to more than one direction, contrary to what we aspire to. The formulation of a single policy by the whole nation on the developments of world policies was affected by difficulties beyond those arising from the fact that there are many Arab states and regimes. The shadow of that situation haunted our policies — policies which good people wanted to be united toward a general direction — although many details of that situation have taken on the local color of our countries.

Based on the above, and in view of other causes, many misgivings, doubts, plots, and harmful actions began to spread among us, to the extent that some Arabs began to race outside the Arab arena toward names, policies, signals, and actions significant to one of the two parties of the conflict. Similarly, our weapons and wills have become burdened — in case of use or nonuse — with the atmosphere of international conflict and its objectives. This, in addition to other factors, hindered agreement on a unified policy among the Arabs. The negative aspects I have mentioned in my statement do not exclude Iraq. Iraq, too, has been affected by the repercussions of the international policy created by the state of polarization, in accordance with its location and characteristics. We have become divided, even in names. Or it might be that we have divided ourselves in this way by various descriptions — leftist, rightist, reactionary, progressive — according to international terminology. Thus, an odious, divisionist psychological state was created, instead of our

Arab policy being built on the single bridge of a unified nation. The principles of Arab nationalism of our time-honored nation — our chivalrous, pan-Arab bonds — that are stirred in our minds and hearts by usurped Palestine have remained constant, although other elements and factors played a frequent role adding to elements of disagreement and dispute. These elements and factors, however, have not been destined to remain constant in view of the force of countercurrents and reactions which we have earlier referred to.

Now, after the removal of the nightmare of the odious division of the world and the conflict that weakened the crystallization of a single human stance on the issues of humanity — which was a stumbling block in the face of national and pan-Arab stands that are basically related to the uniqueness of their circumstances and capabilities — human beings today have opportunities for a new state of being, a genuine consolidation, in addition to other gains. These opportunities will open to the Arabs the broader range of a unified, more constant Arab policy if they know how to deal positively with the developments of international policy and its points of strength, and if they know how to diminish — if not ward off completely — the negative results of these surprising developments. Thus, anyone who has had reason to be influenced by the policy of polarization should quickly abandon his previous position. We will address this call, and we will ask you if you think that your country, Iraq, was affected, or is currently under the influence of, any policies of polarization countries.

We have to maintain a balanced policy based on the interests of the nation and the peoples of our countries in accordance with the relationship between nationalism and pan-Arabism. Otherwise, we will all taste bitterness or sink amid the negative aspects and confusion of world politics without taking advantage of any of its positive aspects. If this occurs, God forbid, the fault will not be with our nation or peoples, but with us, the officials who assume full responsibility at the level of governments as well as the political and popular currents of our nation in the Arab homeland.

Regarding the relationship with Iran, you know, O brothers, that we have chosen peace — as Arabs, not only in Iraq — with all world nations and states, particularly with the nations and states neighboring the Arab homeland. Among these is Iran. This was also our policy before the war, from the very first day of it, and until the day preceding the cease-fire.

We have stressed this position in tangible initiatives, the latest of which is the present exchange of messages between us and Iran, which we hope would lead to a direct and deep dialogue leading to comprehensive peace. In this way we hope to preserve the inalienable rights of all parties, to entrench the principle of noninterference in other countries' domestic affairs, to respect each other's options in accordance with a policy that cannot change with desires and circumstances so that the door of evil and its flame can be closed forever by building sound relations between the Arab nation and the Iranian peoples.

Glory and mercy to Arabism's martyrs everywhere. Glory to the people of the occupied land in Palestine and to their just struggle against the Zionist aggression and occupation. God is great and glory to the Arabs. May God preserve you and guide our steps on the path of honest brotherhood and humanity — steps emphasized by the principles and values of our true religion, for which God chose a prophet from our nation, in order to communicate it to humanity. May God protect you, O brothers and honorable audience. Men said to them: "A great army is gathering against you," and frightened them, but it only increased their faith. They said: "For us God is sufficient, and he is the best disposer of affairs" (Koranic verse). Peace be upon you.

Source: FBIS-NES-90-103, 29 May 1990.

5. Excerpts From Iraqi Transcript of Meeting With US Envoy 25 July 1990

On 25 July 1990 President Saddam Husayn of Iraq summoned the United States ambassador to Baghdad, April Glaspie, to his office in the last high-level contact between the two governments before the Iraqi invasion of Kuwait on 2 August. Following are excerpts from a document described by Iraqi Government officials as a transcript of the meeting, which also included the Iraqi foreign minister, Tariq 'Aziz. A copy was provided to The New York Times by ABC News, which translated it from the Arabic. The State Department has declined to comment on its accuracy. *The New York Times,* 23 September 1990.

Saddam Husayn: I have summoned you today to hold comprehensive political discussions with you. This is a message to President Bush.

You know that we did not have relations with the US until 1984 and you know the circumstances and reasons which caused them to be severed. The decision to establish relations with the US [was] taken in 1980 during the two months prior to the war between us and Iran.

When the war started, and to avoid misinterpretation, we postponed the establishment of relations, hoping that the war would end soon.

But because the war lasted for a long time, and to emphasize the fact that we are a non-aligned country, it was important to re-establish relations with the US. And we chose to do this in 1984.

It is natural to say that the US is not like Britain, for example, with the latter's historic relations with Middle Eastern countries, including Iraq. In addition, there were no relations between Iraq and the US between 1967 and 1984. One can conclude it would be difficult for the US to have a full understanding of many matters in

Iraq. When relations were re-established we hoped for a better understanding and for better cooperation because we too do not understand the background of many American decisions.

We dealt with each other during the war and we had dealings on various levels. The most important of those levels were with the foreign ministers.

US-Iraq Rifts

We had hoped for a better common understanding and a better chance of cooperation to benefit both our peoples and the rest of the Arab nations.

But these better relations have suffered from various rifts. The worst of these was in 1986, only two years after establishing relations, with what was known as Irangate, which happened during the year that Iran occupied the Faw peninsula.

It was natural then to say that old relations and complexity of interests could absorb many mistakes. But when interests are limited and relations are not that old, then there isn't a deep understanding and mistakes could leave a negative effect. Sometimes the effect of an error can be larger than the error itself.

Despite all of that, we accepted the apology, via his envoy, of the American President regarding Irangate, and we wiped the slate clean. And we shouldn't unearth the past except when new events remind us that old mistakes were not just a matter of coincidence.

Our suspicions increased after we liberated the Faw peninsula. The media began to involve itself in our politics. And our suspicions began to surface anew, because we began to question whether the US felt uneasy with the outcome of the war when we liberated our land.

It was clear to us that certain parties in the United States — and I don't say the President himself — but certain parties who had links with the intelligence community and with the State Department — and I don't say the Secretary of State himself — I say that these parties did not like the fact that we liberated our land. Some parties began to prepare studies entitled, "Who will succeed Saddam Husayn?" They began to contact Gulf states to make them fear Iraq,

to persuade them not to give Iraq economic aid. And we have evidence of these activities.

Iraq Policy on Oil

Iraq came out of the war burdened with $40 billion debts, excluding the aid given by Arab states, some of whom consider that too, to be a debt although they knew — and you knew too — that without Iraq they would not have had these sums and the future of the region would have been entirely different.

We began to face the policy of the drop in the price of oil. Then we saw the United States, which always talks of democracy but which has no time for the other point of view. Then the media campaign against Saddam Husayn was started by the official American media. The United States thought that the situation in Iraq was like Poland, Romania or Czechoslovakia. We were disturbed by this campaign but we were not disturbed too much because we had hoped that, in a few months, those who are decision makers in America would have a chance to find the facts and see whether this media campaign had had any effect on the lives of Iraqis. We had hoped that soon the American authorities would make the correct decision regarding their relations with Iraq. Those with good relations can sometimes afford to disagree.

But when planned and deliberate policy forces the price of oil down without good commercial reasons, then that means another war against Iraq. Because military war kills people by bleeding them, and economic war kills their humanity by depriving them of their chance to have a good standard of living. As you know, we gave rivers of blood in a war that lasted eight years, but we did not lose our humanity. Iraqis have a right to live proudly. We do not accept that anyone could injure Iraqi pride or the Iraqi right to have high standards of living.

Kuwait and the UAE were at the front of this policy aimed at lowering Iraq's position and depriving its people of higher economic standards. And you know that our relations with the Emirates and Kuwait had been good. On top of all that, while we were busy at war, the state of Kuwait began to expand at the expense of our territory.

You may say this is propaganda, but I would direct you to one document, the Military Patrol Line, which is the borderline endorsed by the Arab League in 1961 for military patrols not to cross the Iraq-Kuwait border.

But go and look for yourselves. You will see the Kuwaiti border patrols, the Kuwaiti farms, the Kuwaiti oil installations — all built as closely as possible to this line to establish that land as Kuwaiti territory.

Conflicting Interests

Since then, the Kuwaiti Government has been stable while the Iraqi Government has undergone many changes. Even after 1968 and for 10 years afterwards, we were too busy with our own problems. First in the north, then the 1973 war, and other problems. Then came the war with Iran which started 10 years ago.

We believe that the United States must understand that people who live in luxury and economic security can reach an understanding with the United States on what are legitimate joint interests. But the starved and the economically deprived cannot reach the same understanding.

We do not accept threats from anyone because we do not threaten anyone. But we say clearly that we hope that the US will not entertain too many illusions and will seek new friends rather than increase the number of its enemies.

I have read the American statements speaking of friends in the area. Of course, it is the right of everyone to choose their friends. We can have no objections. But you know you are not the ones who protected your friends during the war with Iran. I assure you, had the Iranians overrun the region, the American troops would not have stopped them, except by the use of nuclear weapons.

I do not belittle you. But I hold this view by looking at the geography and [taking the] nature of American society into account. Yours is a society which cannot accept 10,000 dead in one battle.

You know that Iran agreed to the cease-fire not because the United States had bombed one of the oil platforms after the liberation of Faw. Is this Iraq's reward for its role in securing the stability of the region and for protecting it from an unknown flood?

Protecting the Oil Flow

So what can it mean when America says it will now protect its friends? It can only mean prejudice against Iraq. This stance plus maneuvers and statements which have been made has encouraged the UAE and Kuwait to disregard Iraqi rights.

I say to you clearly that Iraq's rights, which are mentioned in the memorandum, we will take one by one. That might not happen now or after a month or after one year, but we will take it all. We are not the kind of people who will relinquish their rights. There is no historic right, or legitimacy, or need, for the UAE and Kuwait to deprive us of our rights. rights. If they are needy, we too are needy.

The United States must have a better understanding of the situation and declare who it wants to have relations with and who its enemies are. But it should not make enemies simply because others have different points of view regarding the Arab-Israeli conflict.

We clearly understand America's statement that it wants an easy flow of oil. We understand America saying that it seeks friendship with the states in the region, and to encourage their joint interests. But we cannot understand the attempt to encourage some parties to harm Iraq's interests.

The United States wants to secure the flow of oil. This is understandable and known. But it must not deploy methods which the United States says it disapproves of — flexing muscles and pressure.

If you use pressure, we will deploy pressure and force. We know that you can harm us although we do not threaten you. But we too can harm you. Everyone can cause harm according to their ability and their size. We cannot come all the way to you in the United States, but individual Arabs may reach you.

War and Friendship

You can come to Iraq with aircraft and missiles but do not push us to the point where we cease to care. And when we feel that you want to injure our pride and take away the Iraqis' chance of a high standard of living, then we will cease to care and death will be the choice for us. Then we would not care if you fired 100 missiles for each missile we fired. Because without pride life would have no value.

It is not reasonable to ask our people to bleed rivers of blood for eight years [and] then to tell them, "Now you have to accept aggression from Kuwait, the UAE or from the US or from Israel."

We do not put all these countries in the same boat. First, we are hurt and upset that such disagreement is taking place between us and Kuwait and the UAE. The solution must be found within an Arab framework and through direct bilateral relations. We do not place America among the enemies. We place it where we want our friends to be and we try to be friends. But repeated American statements last year made it apparent that America did not regard us as friends. Well, the Americans are free.

When we seek friendship we want pride, liberty and our right to choose.

We want to deal according to our status as we deal with the others according to their status.

We consider the others' interests while we look after our own. And we expect the others to consider our interests while they are dealing with their own. What does it mean when the Zionist war minister is summoned to the United States now? What do they mean, these fiery statements coming out of Israel during the past few days and the talk of war being expected now more than at any other time?

I do not believe that anyone would lose by making friends with Iraq. In my opinion, the American President has not made mistakes regarding the Arabs, although his decision to freeze dialogue with the PLO was wrong. But it appears that this decision was made to appease the Zionist lobby or as a piece of strategy to cool the Zionist anger, before trying again. I hope that our latter conclusion is the correct one. But we will carry on saying it was the wrong decision.

You are appeasing the usurper in so many ways — economically, politically, and militarily as well as in the media. When will the time come when, for every three appeasements to the usurper, you praise the Arabs just once?

* * *

April Glaspie: I thank you, Mr. President, and it is a great pleasure for a diplomat to meet and talk directly with the President. I clearly understand your message. We studied history at school. They taught us to say freedom or death. I think you know well that we as a people have our experience with the colonialists.

Mr. President, you mentioned many things during this meeting which I cannot comment on on behalf of my Government. But with your permission, I will comment on two points. You spoke of friendship and I believe it was clear from the letters sent by our President to you on the occasion of your National Day that he emphasizes —

Husayn: He was kind and his expressions met with our regard and respect.

Directive on Relations

Glaspie: As you know, he directed the United States Administration to reject the suggestion of implementing trade sanctions.

Husayn: There is nothing left for us to buy from America. Only wheat. Because every time we want to buy something, they say it is forbidden, I am afraid that one day you will say, "You are going to make gunpowder out of wheat."

Glaspie: I have a direct instruction from the President to seek better relations with Iraq.

Husayn: But how? We too have this desire. But matters are running contrary to this desire.

Glaspie: This is less likely to happen the more we talk. For example, you mentioned the issue of the article published by the American Information Agency and that was sad. And a formal apology was presented.

Husayn: Your stance is generous. We are Arabs. It is enough for us that someone says, "I am sorry, I made a mistake." Then we carry on. But the media campaign continued. And it is full of stories. If the stories were true, no one would get upset. But we understand from its continuation that there is a determination.

Glaspie: I saw the Diane Sawyer program on ABC. And what happened in that program was cheap and unjust. And this is a real picture of what happens in the American media — even to American politicians themselves. These are the methods the Western media employs. I am pleased that you add your voice to the diplomats who stand up to the media. Because your appearance in the media, even for five minutes, would help us to make the American people understand Iraq. This would increase mutual understanding. If the American President had control of the media, his job would be much easier.

Mr. President, not only do I want to say that President Bush wanted better and deeper relations with Iraq, but he also wants an Iraqi contribution to peace and prosperity in the Middle East. President Bush is an intelligent man. He is not going to declare an economic war against Iraq.

You are right. It is true what you say that we do not want higher prices for oil. But I would ask you to examine the possibility of not charging too high a price for oil.

Husayn: We do not want too high prices for oil. And I remind you that in 1974 I gave Tariq 'Aziz the idea for an article he wrote which criticized the policy of keeping oil prices high. It was the first Arab article which expressed this view.

Shifting Price of Oil

Tariq 'Aziz: Our policy in OPEC opposes sudden jumps in oil prices.

Husayn: Twenty-five dollars a barrel is not a high price.

Glaspie: We have many Americans who would like to see the price go above $25 because they come from oil-producing states.

Husayn: The price at one stage had dropped to $12 a barrel and a reduction in the modest Iraqi budget of $6 billion to $7 billion is a disaster.

Glaspie: I think I understand this. I have lived here for years. I admire your extraordinary efforts to rebuild your country. I know you need funds. We understand that and our opinion is that you should have the opportunity to rebuild your country. But we have no opinion on the Arab-Arab conflicts, like your border disagreement with Kuwait.

I was in the American Embassy in Kuwait during the late 60s. The instruction we had during this period was that we should express no opinion on this issue and that the issue is not associated with America. James Baker has directed our official spokesmen to emphasize this instruction. We hope you can solve this problem using any suitable methods via Klibi or via President Mubarak. All that we hope is that these issues are solved quickly. With regard to all of this, can I ask you to see how the issue appears to us?

My assessment after 25 years' service in this area is that your objective must have strong backing from your Arab brothers. I now speak of oil. But you, Mr. President, have fought through a horrific and painful war. Frankly, we can only see that you have deployed massive troops in the south. Normally that would not be any of our business. But when this happens in the context of what you said on your National Day, then when we read the details in the two letters of the Foreign Minister, then when we see the Iraqi point of view that the measures taken by the UAE and Kuwait is, in the final analysis, parallel to military aggression against Iraq, then it would be reasonable for me to be concerned. And for this reason, I received an instruction to ask you, in the spirit of friendship — not in the spirit of confrontation — regarding your intentions.

I simply describe the concern of my Government. And I do not mean that the situation is a simple situation. But our concern is a simple one.

Husayn: We do not ask people not to be concerned when peace is at issue. This is a noble human feeling which we all feel. It is natural for you as a superpower to be concerned. But what we ask is not to express your concern in a way that would make an aggressor believe that he is getting support for his aggression.

We want to find a just solution which will give us our rights but not deprive others of their rights. But at the same time, we want the others to know that our patience is running out regarding their action, which is harming even the milk our children drink, and the pensions of the widow who lost her husband during the war, and the pensions of the orphans who lost their parents.

As a country, we have the right to prosper. We lost so many opportunities, and the others should value the Iraqi role in their protection. Even this Iraqi (the President points to the interpreter) feels bitter like all other Iraqis. We are not aggressors but we do not accept aggression either. We sent them envoys and handwritten letters. We tried everything. We asked the Servant of the Two Shrines — King Fahd — to hold a four-member summit, but he suggested a meeting between the Oil Ministers. We agreed. And as you know, the meeting took place in Jidda. They reached an agreement which did not express what we wanted, but we agreed.

Only two days after the meeting, the Kuwaiti Oil Minister made a statement that contradicted the agreement. We also discussed the issue during the Baghdad summit. I told the Arab Kings and Presidents that some brothers are fighting an economic war against us. And that not all wars use weapons and we regard this kind of war as a military action against us. Because if the capability of our army is lowered then, if Iran renewed the war, it could achieve goals which it could not achieve before. And if we lowered the standard of our defenses, then this could encourage Israel to attack us. I said that before the Arab Kings and Presidents. Only I did not mention Kuwait and UAE by name, because they were my guests.

Before this, I had sent them envoys reminding them that our war had included their defense. Therefore the aid they gave us should not be regarded as a debt. We did no more than the United States would have done against someone who attacked its interests.

I talked about the same thing with a number of other Arab states. I explained the situation to brother King Fahd a few times, by sending envoys and on the telephone. I talked with brother King Husayn and with Shaykh Zayd after the conclusion of the summit. I walked with the Shaykh to the plane when he was leaving Mosul. He told me, "Just wait until I get home." But after he had reached his

destination, the statements that came from there were very bad —
not from him, but from his Minister of Oil.

Also after the Jidda agreement, we received some intelligence that
they were talking of sticking to the agreement for two months only.
Then they would change their policy. Now tell us, if the American
President found himself in this situation, what would he do? I said it
was very difficult for me to talk about these issues in public. But we
must tell the Iraqi people who face economic difficulties who was
responsible for that.

Talks With Mubarak

Glaspie: I spent four beautiful years in Egypt.

Husayn: The Egyptian people are kind and good and ancient. The
oil people are supposed to help the Egyptian people, but they are
mean beyond belief. It is painful to admit it, but some of them are
disliked by Arabs because of their greed.

Glaspie: Mr. President, it would be helpful if you could give us an
assessment of the effort made by your Arab brothers and whether
they have achieved anything.

Husayn: On this subject, we agreed with President Mubarak that
the Prime Minister of Kuwait would meet with the deputy chairman
of the Revolution Command Council in Saudi Arabia, because the
Saudis initiated contact with us, aided by President Mubarak's
efforts. He just telephoned me a short while ago to say the Kuwaitis
have agreed to that suggestion.

Glaspie: Congratulations.

Husayn: A protocol meeting will be held in Saudi Arabia. Then
the meeting will be transferred to Baghdad for deeper discussion
directly between Kuwait and Iraq. We hope we will reach some
result. We hope that the long-term view and the real interests will
overcome Kuwaiti greed.

Glaspie: May I ask you when you expect Shaykh Sa'd to come to
Baghdad?

Husayn: I suppose it would be on Saturday or Monday at the
latest. I told brother Mubarak that the agreement should be in
Baghdad Saturday or Sunday. You know that brother Mubarak's
visits have always been a good omen.

Glaspie: This is good news. Congratulations.

Husayn: Brother President Mubarak told me they were scared. They said troops were only 20 kilometers north of the Arab League line. I said to him that regardless of what is there, whether they are police, border guards or army, and regardless of how many are there, and what they are doing, assure the Kuwaitis and give them our word that we are not going to do anything until we meet with them. When we meet and when we see that there is hope, then nothing will happen. But if we are unable to find a solution, then it will be natural that Iraq will not accept death, even though wisdom is above everything else. There you have good news.

'Aziz: This is a journalistic exclusive.

Glaspie: I am planning to go to the United States next Monday. I hope I will meet with President Bush in Washington next week. I thought to postpone my trip because of the difficulties we are facing. But now I will fly on Monday.

Source: The New York Times International, 23 September 1990.

6. Saddam Husayn Issues "Victory Day" Message
7 August 1990

Message from President Saddam Husayn "on the occasion of the great victory day on 8 August 1988" — read by announcer. *Baghdad Domestic Service in Arabic 1700 GMT, 7 August 1990.*

In the name of God, the merciful, the compassionate.

O great Iraqi people, O sons of the glorious Arab nation, on 8 August 1988 matters were settled after eight years of dueling. That day was the day of days, and the communiqué that was issued on that day was the communiqué of communiqués. That day was truly the day of days because every day, beginning with the first day in the book of the second al- Qadisiyya that began on 4 September 1980 and ending with the last day of that eternal and great book of our people's life that preceded the day of days on 7 August 1988 has a share in the day of 8 August 1988. The communiqué broadcast on 8 August was the communiqué of communiqués because every communiqué issued from 4 September 1980 to 7 August 1988 is a vital part of the fruits of the record from which the banner of victory was raised high on 8 August 1988. From this we can see the peoples' record, and history cannot exist without the accumulation of repeated sacrifices, wisdom, bravery, patient work, and true struggle to God's satisfaction. By this we can see that the day of days began from the first day of the record and that the communiqué of communiqués was written in the first communiqué of the second al-Qadisiyya.

The day of days gives lessons to those who heed them, lessons whose meanings and dimensions go beyond the national borders to affect the entire nation and humanity at large. There are people who do not benefit from other people's lessons and there are those who do benefit. All this is determined by the fact that some leaders draw lessons in accordance with the patriotic and national aspects of human wisdom and some others learn the lessons they wish — but not the truth as it is.

We do not like lessons outside the course of life, except those affiliated with God. We do not give reason the full right to interpret things independently from the eye or give the eye the full right apart from reason. The two should cooperate in concrete and abstract matters. The blood of our martyrs has turned into a permanent torch along our people's path toward progress and a better life. The edifice of progress is rising with the passing of every day since 8 August 1988, and its foundation is becoming stronger on the basis of righteousness and justice. Mistakes in its course are being dealt with on the basis of the insistence of the people, who have defended rights and justice and offered sacrifices for them. Thus, the people deserve a life that is not disturbed by evil intentions, and the torch lit by the martyrs' blood that represents virtue and national and pan-Arab dignity should not be extinguished by the attempts of non-patriots, non-nationalists, and non-humanitarians.

Therefore, the day of days and the communiqué of communiqués became not the end of a stage in the life of the Iraqis and the nation, but the serious beginning of a life of honor and triumph in all walks of life — in theory and practice — as well as in the arena of the battlefield whenever the heat rises.

Therefore, we have the right and it is our duty to say that the day of the call, the second of this month, August, in this year, is the legitimate newborn child of 8 August 1988. In fact, this is the only way to deal with these despicable Croesuses* who relished stealing the part to harm the whole, who relished possession to destroy devotion, and who were guided by the foreigner instead of being guided by virtuous standards, principles of pan-Arabism, and the creed of humanitarianism in relations between the sons of the same people and nation. The second of August was a day bursting with these meanings. In the same way it is the legitimate newborn child of the struggle, patience, and perseverance of the Kuwaiti people, which was crowned by revolutionary action on that immortal day.

The newborn child was born of a legitimate father and an immaculate mother. It will be a loyal son to the Kuwaitis, Iraqis, and all the Arabs. Greetings to the makers of the second of August, whose efforts God has blessed. They have achieved one of the brightest, most promising, and most principled national and pan-Arab acts.

At a time when the second of August arrived to be the legitimate newborn son of the second Qadisiyya and its people — and with God's help, it will also be a loyal son — it and its consequences shall be the beginning of a new, lofty, and rising stage in which virtue will spread throughout the Arab homeland in the coming days and

---

*   In the Arabic source the Qarun of Kuwait — after the Pharaoh's greedy, corrupt and oppressive vizier who according to the Koran was swallowed up by the ground.

profanity, treachery, betrayal, meanness, and subservience to the foreigner will retreat from it. Many of the goals of the Arabs will move closer after some believed they were moving away from their places in the horizon. New suns and moons will shine, stars will glitter, light will expel darkness, and lunar and solar eclipses will withdraw from the skies of Iraq and the Arab world.

How can that be?

When the sun of the Arabs set in its faraway horizon, after Baghdad's eye was put out and its mind was ruined by the actions and rule of the foreigner, a pitch-black darkness prevailed throughout the Arab world, with the exception of local cases that used to emerge here and there and every now and then under certain symptoms and whose indications were not wholly pan-Arab. The Arabs had no sun, moon or stars to guide them to any road with a glimmer of hope.

When they saw before them the opportunity to be liberated from the darkness of the Ottoman era, and the virtuous and patriotic Arabs determined to change the image of the state of the Arabs, they fell into the claws of the forces of the age as soon as they took their first step. At a time when some foreign rulers were overthrown by Arab rulers to start with, and liberation revolutions and movements took place after the first Arab revolution to replace what was left with local, national, or pan-Arab alternatives, the partition and dispersion of the factors of power and capability throughout various regions retained a weak Arab homeland — weak individuals, actions, and aspirations. In this condition, every time the Arab took a step forward, he took two steps back, or a bit more or a bit less than that step, and was moved further away from the position he was supposed to be in.

The malicious Westerners, while partitioning the Arab homeland, intentionally multiplied the number of countries with the result that the Arab nation could not achieve the integration needed to realize its full capability. In this way, they also fragmented capabilities. While fragmenting the Arab homeland, they intentionally distanced the majority of the population density and areas of cultural depth from riches and their sources, something new to the life of Arabs.

This became one of the most dangerous results of partition and a fatal wedge in Arab relations.

The wealth centered in one place, in the hands of a minority lacking in cultural depth or, more accurately, having no record of cultural depth. On the other hand, cultural depth and population density centered in a place remote from the sources of the new wealth, as I said. This malicious act resulted in the minority becoming so corrupt that it was cut off from its nation. It stopped mentioning this nation, except in lip service and on some ceremonial occasions. The wealth in the hands of this minority did not come as a result of legitimate hard work. The overwhelming majority of the nation, which was living away from the sources of wealth and enduring a major part of its negative impact on its life in the social, psychological, cultural, military, and political spheres, suffered a weakness that, if not overcome, could not allow this majority to play a vital and effective role in the life of the nation.

The authority of the honorable national and pan-Arab majority and its leading influence on the Arab life was absent and was replaced by the authority of the corrupt minority, which is connected with the foreigner. As a result, the nation was hit right between the eyes, and the damage it suffered was no less in its consequences than direct foreign rule. Indeed, at some stages of the nation's life direct foreign rule awakened — through reaction — the national and pan-Arab awareness and crystallized the factors of spiritual upsurge in which the nation invoked its genuine values from the depths of its culture.

But the nation's situation before 2 August this year was fatal to its soul and body. One could not but feel its descent into the abyss. This situation would rob rulers and people of their courage, whether among the corrupt wealthy minority or among the overwhelming majority of the poor Arabs. It would also block the capable collective efforts in the two places, make the people in both places dependent on foreigners in one way or another, and seriously upset the social life in both places. Moreover, efforts toward true interaction with the laws of the age would become absent or weak, and, consequently, the process of formulating these laws in a national and pan-Arab manner would be hindered in both places. Furthermore, the nation — in its cultural sense, collective capability, and joint action — would become lacking in both areas. The nation will return to its rightful position only through real struggle and jihad to place the wealth of the nation in the service of its noble objectives so that the opinion of the majority would become prevalent, capable, and honest, and the opinion of the minority will be respected when it is honest. Its conduct, then, will be remote from decay and corruption.

Two August has come as a very violent response to the harm that the foreigner has wanted to perpetrate against Iraq and the nation. The Croesus of Kuwait and his aides became the obedient, humiliated, and treacherous dependents of that foreigner. Instead of honoring its commitments toward the stem, the dead branch began stabbing the stem with a poisonous dagger in the back so that it might fall dead beside the dead branch and so that the living stem would not try to awaken the dead branch (sentence as heard). What took place on 2 August was inevitable so that death might not prevail over life, so that those who were capable of ascending to the peak would not be brought down to the abysmal precipice, so that corruption and remoteness from God would not spread to the majority as a result of need and poverty after the corrupt minority had distanced itself from God, values, books, and disciples. Honor will be kept in Mesopotamia so that Iraq will continue to be the pride of the Arabs, their protector, and their model of noble values, and so that Kuwait will join the march of its nation.

The lowly wanted and planned to harm the free women of Iraq, as they had done to free Arab women in other places. But their calculations went wrong because they did not know that we prefer death to this and that we cannot sleep without putting out the eyes of those who encroach upon Iraqi and Arab and Islamic values. Death is better than humiliation and subordination to the foreigner.

This was the 8th of August 1988, the day of days, in which the communiqué of communiqués was issued, declaring the great victory. It will be the fountainhead of all the sweet days in the life of the Arabs, and their compassionate mother, as was the day of 2 August this year.

Glory to the martyrs; glory to the free, living people; God is great; and accursed be the lowly.

(Signed) Saddam Husayn, 16 Muharram, 1411 Hegira, corresponding to 7 August 1990.

Source: FBIS-NES-90-153, 8 August 1990.

7. Saddam Husayn Addresses National Assembly
7 August 1990

Speech by President Saddam Husayn to the National Assembly on 7 August 1990 in Baghdad — recorded. *Baghdad Domestic Service in Arabic 1653 GMT, 8 August 1990.*

In the name of God, the merciful, the compassionate. Brother men and women who are representing their valiant people, the best representation, the days are not equal in their meanings and sacrifices. It is not at a single juncture of life that man achieves the dreams he has cherished. However, while speaking to you, I feel all the depth of national and pan-Arab human feelings. The moment we are experiencing today under this dome will give shape to its meanings in light of the decisions you make and the opinions you express. Likewise, other places where we have met with our brothers in the Revolution Command Council, the Regional Command, and the Provisional Free Kuwait Government will have their historical meaning.

When a decision that is made at the spur of the moment is to be considered historic, its effects and present and future meanings will have to be different from those of other decisions. You are today, like all the great Iraqi people, before a new historical juncture. The word juncture might be found in usual political speeches. Today, however, the word extends to cover its profound and full sense. The word today means the new will and the new future. It means determination, resolve, and will, whereby we should put things right so that Iraq will go forward and the banners of victory will flutter everywhere, and so that Iraq will be the new launching base for all the Arab free men wherever they might be — the Arabs who have long cherished dreams on the road of unity, progress, and liberation.

This is what is before you to debate today, brothers; it is the return of dear Kuwait to its kinfolk in al-Najaf, Karbala. We are supposed to decide and appreciate the value of decision, when Kuwait is returned to its kinsfolk in al-Najaf, in Karbala, in Baghdad, in Kirkuk, in Nineve, and to all our dear people wherever they are — in Sulaymaniyya, in Irbid, in Dohuk, in Salah al-Din, in al-Basrah, and all the dear cities of Iraq. Kuwait is joining the motherland just as are al-Jahra, al-Ahmadi, and all the villages, and all the good people and the good land that was detached from Iraq some time ago and whose human and national essence was assassinated wherever the foreigner was able to assassinate. There remained enough of this generous essence, though, to decide to return to the lap of its generous mother. Brothers, representatives of the people, this is what you have to discuss, and this is the letter of the Provisional Free Government to the leadership in Iraq, to you, and the people stating that Kuwait is the branch, as historical facts prove (applause), and that Iraq is the land.

In their message, they appealed to Iraq to approve this decision. In a joint meeting of the RCC and the Regional Command, because the Provisional Free Government in cherished Kuwait asked that unity take the form of a comprehensive merger out of commitment and loyalty to the correct historical roots that Kuwait and Iraq have — one existence — the RCC, the Ba'th Party Regional Command, and the Council of Ministers unanimously agreed, as well as the Council of Ministers of the Provisional Government of beloved Kuwait, that Iraq and Kuwait become the manifestation of a full merger (applause). Despite the fact that your emotions are a clear and indisputable decision, I leave the National Assembly speaker here with you for you to make the decision in accordance with the law, in light of what you have heard from me so that we can hear your opinion in the form of a draft resolution later on.

I say, this is a final decision. It is a decision for good. It is a decision for the Iraqi people to become comprehensive in the true meaning of the word, on their territory and its extensions. Those who try to obstruct this decision from outside Iraq, will, with God's help, reap disappointment, defeat, and shame (applause, chanting of patriotic verse).

Along with this decision and the new Iraq, there is a clear gain for every honorable Arab wherever he may be and for every noble nationalist in all corners of the Arab world; for every widow whose husband has struggled for freedom, for Jerusalem, for Palestine, and for dignity and honor; for every orphan there is also a gain. It is a gain against the behavior of corrupt and despotic people who have no other concern than to parade Arab women in some parts of the Arab homeland. They have no worry but to squander the people's money.

The time has come for the truth to emerge in a blaze of light. This march will not bow except before God, the lord of the skies and the earth. Its banner will be brought down. The new Iraq with its 18 million, 19 million, will be capable of fighting the enemies regardless of their number, with God's help.

We neither commit aggression nor cherish aggression. But whoever attacks us will most certainly regret it and will curse his bad luck later. The will of Iraq will remain lofty, proud, and strong. The men of Iraq from the land, from Zakhu, to the sea, to al-Ahmadi and Kuwait (applause), will remain dear and lofty. Virtues will be their guide so that darkness will be defeated forever and so that the sun of Iraq will remain shining forever, God willing.

Source: FBIS-NES-90-154, 9 August 1990.

8. RCC Approves "Merger" Decision With Kuwait
8 August 1990

Statement issued by the Iraqi Revolution Command Council (RCC), on 8 August 1990 — read by announcer. *Baghdad Domestic Service in Arabic 1436 GMT, 8 August 1990.*

In the name of God, the merciful, the compassionate. O great Iraqi people from the land to the sea, O zealous Arabs everywhere: scarce are the days when the Arabs are jubilant, when they are joyous because of the meanings these days carry, and when they look forward to the days to come. This has been the situation of the Arabs for the long time in which the foreigner reigned, when the national and pan-Arab will became absent from the seat of government. This had been their situation when national rule began and spread all over the homeland, because although the foreigner has abandoned the formulas of direct colonialism which it had previously adopted, it has not departed from within our ranks through its agents and intrigues. One of the most egregious criminal acts of colonialism was its partition of the homeland, which was a single homeland the day Baghdad was the capital of all Arabs.

Following the independence Arab countries won, imperialism started intensifying its malicious actions. Thus, it partitioned many countries in harmony with the calculations of its aims and objectives to undermine the capabilities of the countries that have acquired a civilized depth and power to act and look forward to an effective national role, not only within their defined areas but also in the entire area of the Arab homeland and the Arab nation in its entirety. Thus, the spiteful pencil and scissors of imperialism began to draw up maps, based on ensuring that every part of the Arab homeland — in case it lives under the entity of an independent state — will remain weak and ineffective toward Arab awakening and unity as a whole and that this action should cast its negative effects and shadows on relations among Arab countries so that infighting and division will replace solidarity and conciliation.

In all cases, while drawing up geographic and sovereignty boundaries for all states, Western colonialism sought to make all states weak and to ensure that partition, with the passage of time, would prevent these states from closing ranks and demonstrating a unified stance. Thus, wherever possible it separated civilization with its high, strong state of preparedness due to the rich culture and demographic density from the resources of the new wealth, petroleum and other minerals, where there is a small population, a lack of cultural depth, and a weak state of preparedness due to the absence of the prerequisites for this.

Thus, colonialism achieved its objectives. The strongest evidence to show its success is that it turned the Arab homeland into 22 states before the launching of the blessed Yemeni unity in May. By pursuing these methods, colonialism divested the Arabs of not only the components of material capabilities but also of the components of spiritual progress. Poverty among the majority was coupled — poverty is akin to infidelity — with the inequity created by the ready wealth, which was not gained gradually by the minority, [a minority] which was not properly prepared to dispose of the wealth that it acquired in excess of balanced human needs, without any effort or persistence. Thus, it corrupted many individuals of this minority, foremost among whom are the rulers. Hence, it robbed them of spiritual values and made them forget about their duties to God and man. What has befallen other states in the Arab lands befell Iraq when colonialism divested it of a dear part of it, namely Kuwait, and kept Iraq away from the waters to prevent it from acquiring part of its tactical and strategic abilities, and thus kept part of its people and part of its wealth away from the origin and the wellspring.

Thanks to the traits of Iraqi individuals and to the nature of the age-old depth of its civilization, and because the resources of the new wealth in it cover all parts of its lands from the north, the central regions, and the south, Western colonialism has not managed to achieve through partition in Iraq what it managed to achieve in other Arab states. Thus, Iraq has remained, with the exception of well-known periods in its march, close to God and its individuals. Therefore, after the great July 1968 revolution, God became present in minds, hearts, and consciences.

From another perspective, the human being generally gained a distinguished status, whether theoretically or in behavior, on both the level of the citizens and leadership, except for that part of it which deviated from the course — Kuwait. Because the gates of the sky open up to the active and goodwill and to the determination of the believers who reject oppression, tyranny, and injustice, the gates of the sky opened up to Iraq before the day of the call on 2 August and to its detached part, Kuwait.

Woe be to those for whom the gates of the sky open up their brightness and who are late in taking that opportunity. Woe be to us from God's torture if we are late in performing our duties toward Him. Some of our duties to Him and on His land are struggle and jihad for the sake of a deep pan-Arab awakening which rectifies affairs and retrieves for the Arab individual his status and leading role in the message of God and life. This cannot be achieved before its correct conditions are achieved, starting with the self. The self we refer to here is a group, national self. Then, the basis of what is right will not be achieved before the part detached from its origin and source is returned. What happened, happened on the day of the call on 2 August.

The day of the call is a great day. The gates of the sky opened up before Iraq, with God's will, and wide opportunities opened up before all the Arabs. However, at the same time and on a par with this opportunity and as one of its conditions, new battlefields were opened up for all the believers against all the infidels. No one is more capable than the al-Qadisiyya people and its leadership of fulfilling this opportunity after taking it.

Based on all this, in response to the appeal in the communiqué of the Provisional Free Kuwait Government stemming from the great transformation that took place in the lives of our people after the day of the call; for reasons of principles, values, and facts brought forth on that glorious day, 2 August of this month, which was blessed by God in the introduction of the Arabs' victory in their second al-Qadisiyya*; in view of what the situation has resulted in after the Croesus entity was shaken and after the earth under its feet and the feet of its collaborators collapsed; with the objective of weakening the hopes of the traitors and evildoers inside and outside the Arab homeland; in order to place issues in their proper perspective by bringing the part and branch, Kuwait, to the whole, origin, and source, Iraq; and to rectify what time had wronged and to cancel the injustice and unfairness that had hit Iraq in the heart of its entity before the day of the call; the RCC has decided to return the part and branch, Kuwait, to the whole and root, Iraq, in a comprehensive, eternal, and inseparable merger unity. In this union there will prevail the same concepts and values prevailing in the other parts of Iraq, which will bolster the unity of Iraq — land, individual, regional waters, and space.

O great Iraqi people, O masses of Arab nation. O Arab leaders, whenever you support the principles of truth and the interests of the Arabs, and whenever you overcome obscurity and selfishness and reject the foreigner's pressure, ways, and ploys, this has been our decision. It is a rightful, just, and fair decision. It is a decision for the present time and for the future. At the same time, after Iraq acted on 2 August along with all its sons to carry out this honorable national duty, this decision is being made for the Arab nation as a whole in view of the power, capability, faith, and aspirations it implies. It is a decision for all Iraqis, from the land to the sea. At the same time, it is for all good Arabs from the Ocean to the Gulf. Having made this decision, we tell all evildoers and conspirators that all fleets, planes, and centers of oppressive forces in the world, whether inside or outside the Arab homeland, will not shake the palm fronds in al-Basra, al-Qadisiyya, al-Muthanna, Kuwait, al-Jahra, and the city of the call, al-Ahamdi. We say to them we will fight your criminal force, whether you threaten us with it or use it in a way that deserves every sacrifice by the militants and strugglers of the Arabs and all the righteous Arabs. The blood of our martyrs will burn you, so that

---

* The second al-Qadisiyya, the name given to the Iraqi-Iranian War.

Iraq will remain glorious and will establish through its glory and the glory of other countries a lofty glory for all the Arabs.

We tell those who are afraid of what they call the Kuwait precedent: You must not be deluded into incorrect measuring of matters; what exists between Iraq and its southern parts in al-Jahra, Kuwait City, and the city of the call is a matter that concerns Iraq. We have no ambitions for territory or for the wealth of anyone. Let those who want to heed lessons do so. We tell those who are trying to assemble the ranks of evil that the many names siding against us will not hide from us the manipulators and the lackeys of hell. The tongues of flame will only further expose their shameless faces. Since the matter is still at the beginning, Iraq is generous, and God is forgiving and merciful. So, let them stop their transgressions against Iraq and remove the venom from their tongues. This is because the continuation of the treacherous plan and preparation for and initiation of aggression will make us accurately monitor the role of every evildoer in this conspiracy. They will not escape but will be taken into account whenever God wishes. Let the Croesus of Kuwait be a lesson to go by instead of being an additional factor for more misguidance, sins, and injustice.

The people of Iraq, as they know, have it in them to make a stand until the victorious end willed by God. Accursed be the lowly. There will be those who will triumph and those who will reap ignominy. The dawn will break and the sun will rise to brighten the paths of darkness and aberration. Iraq is rich in bounties, and the generous people around it are many. Those looking for benefits and trade are also many, and they make their way to Iraq, even if it looks as though an airtight blockade has been imposed on it. The aggression will fail and so will the economic blockade, as well as — God willing and thanks to the resolve of the Iraqis and the Arabs — the military aggression.

After seeking God's forgiveness and help, we will demolish blasphemy with faith. A new dawn has broken in the lives of the Arabs, so that they may add it to what few days they have rejoiced in together, and so that it can act as a beam to dissipate darkness. The dawn has broken to stay, and the bats will have to go back to their caves. God is omnipotent and omnipresent, and while the vicious men do not mind leading lives of humiliation and dependence, the men who will heed his commands would like nothing more than to die when the only option open to them is to die in the cause of God and pass on to their children and grandchildren decent lives. We would tell the foreigners that their accomplices will pay a heavy price and if hostilities should break out, [it] will lead to badges and ranks falling from heads and shoulders, while laurel wreaths will increase, as will the ranks of honor and pride on the heads and shoulders of the chivalrous. God will curse the accursed, and everyone will pay the price of his actions. And the faithful will be rewarded. Say "nothing will happen to us except what God has decreed for us, He is our protector, and in God let the believers put their trust" (Koranic verse). God is great, God is great, God is great; let the lowly be accursed, and God's peace and mercy be upon you, honorable brothers, wherever you are.

(Signed) The Revolution Command Council, 8 August 1990.

Source: FBIS-NES-90-154, 9 August 1990.

9. Saddam Husayn's Speech on "Linkage" c. 12 August 1990

Text of President Saddam Husayn's "initiative on previous and subsequent developments in the region," date not given — read by announcer. *Baghdad Domestic Service in Arabic 1530 GMT, 12 August 1990.*

In the name of God, the merciful, the compassionate. So as to contribute to creating an atmosphere of true peace in the region, to facilitate placing the region in a state of stability, to expose the falsehood of America and its deformed midget ally, Israel, to expose its small agents and their crimes against the nation, and to reaffirm right from a position of strength with faith in God, the people, and the nation, we have decided to propose the following initiative:

The United States has tried to cover its moves, which are hostile to humanity and the region's peoples, on the pretext that the decisions of the economic boycott of Iraq constitute a protest against Iraq's assistance to the people of Kuwait, who have saved themselves from the al-Sabah rule. Then it lost its mind when the Kuwaitis and the Iraqis decided to reconnect what British colonialism severed between Iraq and Kuwait, when Kuwait had been part of Iraq until World War I. Iraq had not recognized the crime perpetrated by colonialism until the present time. Later, the United States began to mass war fleets and aircraft squadrons, and to beat the drums of war against Iraq on the pretext of confronting Iraqi threats to Saudi Arabia. Because the spark of war, if it begins, will burn many people and inflict many catastrophes on those who are in its field; and in order to state facts as they are to world public opinion in general, and Western public opinion in particular, and to expose the falsehood of the assertions of the United States that it supports people's causes and rights, and that it seeks to maintain security and the West's interests only, I propose that all issues of occupation, or the issues that have been depicted as occupation in the entire region, be resolved in accordance with the same bases, principles, and premises to be set by the UN Security Council, as follows:

First, the preparation of withdrawal arrangements in accordance with the same principles for the immediate and unconditional withdrawal of Israel from the occupied Arab territories in Palestine, Syria, and Lebanon, Syria's withdrawal from Lebanon, a withdrawal between Iraq and Iran, the formulation of arrangements for the situation in Kuwait, and the timing of the military arrangements and related political arrangements which must apply to all cases and in accordance with the same bases, principles, and premises, taking into consideration the historical rights of Iraq in its territory and the Kuwaiti people's choice, provided the implementation of the program begins with the oldest occupation, or what was called occupation, beginning with the enforcement of all applicable UN Security Council and UN resolutions, until we get to the most recent occupation, and on condition that the same measures passed by the UN Security Council against Iraq be adopted against any party that fails to obligate itself or comply with this arrangement.

Second, with the purpose of displaying the facts to world public opinion to judge in accordance with objective conditions apart from US wishes and pressure, we propose the immediate withdrawal from Saudi Arabia of US forces and the other forces that responded to its conspiracy. They will be replaced by Arab forces whose number, nationality, duties, and location will be defined by the UN Security Council, assisted by the UN secretary general. The nationality of the military forces between Iraq and Saudi Arabia will also be agreed upon on the condition that the forces of the Government of Egypt, which the United States used in carrying out its plot against the Arab nation, be excluded.

Third, all boycott and siege decisions against Iraq shall be frozen immediately. Matters should return to normal in the economic, political, and scientific dealings between Iraq and the rest of the world. These resolutions should not be discussed and implemented again except when they are violated in light of what is stated above in items one, two, and three.

However, if America and its small agents do not respond to our initiative, we, the good sons of the Arab nation and the great Iraqi people, will strongly resist its evil intentions and aggressive schemes. We will triumph, with God's help, and the evildoers will regret their actions after they leave the region defeated, cursed, and humiliated. God is great, accursed be the lowly.

(Signed) Saddam Husayn, 12 August 1990, corresponding to 21 Muharram 1411 Hegira.

Source: FBIS-NES-90-156, 13 August 1990.

10. Saddam Husayn Responds to Mubarak in "Open Letter"
c. 23 August 1990

"Open letter" from President Saddam Husayn to Egyptian President Husni Mubarak, date not given — read by announcer. *Baghdad Domestic Service in Arabic 1500 GMT, 23 August 1990.*

In the name of God, the merciful, the compassionate.

Mr. Muhammad Husni Mabarak, president of the Arab Republic of Egypt, peace be upon you.

I have been acquainted with the appeal you addressed to us in which you called on the Iraqis to withdraw from Kuwait. You addressed your appeal to us on the basis of what you understand about pan-Arabism and the principles of Islam. Having reread the appeal, I am responding to it. However, my response requires patience from you to read the contents of the answer as well as a degree of tolerance toward the concepts it will contain. This is because the essential points of my answer will appear repetitive because I have mentioned them to you on more than one occasion. You used to approve of them, or thus it seemed to me at least. However, God almighty has taught us a great deal. Or let us say, God has taught a great deal of what should be taught to His slaves, or to those who are prepared to learn. Needless to say, the good slaves of God are more capable of learning what should and must be learned. This is because their faith goes beyond pure mental ability as a basic element for learning and assimilation. Among what we have learned from the book of God, the holy Koran, is God's adoption of dialogue with man and His extreme care about it. Wherever God found that man's faith was uncertain or disobeyed the orders of God and His role in creation, He provided him with evidence that removed the uncertainty of monotheism and misguidance, approaching him with a style of dialogue whose level we humans have not been up to. Thus, God tells man: Bring your convincing proof (part of Koranic verse). If God almighty, as a path to faith, leaving for man the option of being guided to faith or not, adopts dialogue and calls on those who have other beliefs, bring your convincing proof, we should do so, as God's slaves, to avoid trying to prove what we consider facts or what is deemed an accusation without proof. On the basis of these great human concepts, I must embark on a dialogue with you before I say yes or no about all that your letter contained and all that is a topic of dialogue, discussion, and argument in Egypt, the Arab homeland, and even the world.

Your Excellency the President, before God bestowed on us or before circumstances created the events until we reached the presidency of the republic of Iraq and you became the head authority in Egypt, we were normal citizens. This speaker (Saddam Husayn), the slave of God, was the son of a peasant who died months before his (Saddam Husayn's) mother gave birth to him. He is from an honorable family whose honor is basically derived from its labor and from being a descendant of the Muhammadist Qurayshi (the tribe of Prophet Muhammad) family, as his family's lineage goes back to our master and forefather, al-Husayn, who is the son of 'Ali Bin Abi Talib (Prophet Muhammad's cousin and husband of one of the prophet's daughters).

To the best of my knowledge, you, Mr. President, have come of an Egyptian family that has nothing to do with the princes and kings who ruled before the July 1952 revolution. At any rate, by virtue of the fact that we are part of the people, I suppose that our becoming presidents should not make us forget about the people's life, particularly considering that we are responsible for our people, each in accordance with his own position. Besides, we are also responsible for the nation, each according to his belief. Some of these responsibilities are constitutional, which is the epithet for our official responsibilities. The humble servant of God who is addressing you has taken it upon himself to shoulder another responsibility according to which he began to act before he rose to positions of responsibility — since he was a schoolboy. Saddam Husayn believes that the Arab nation is a single nation, that the Arab homeland from the Atlantic Ocean to the Arabian Gulf is a single homeland, that Muhammad Bin 'Abdallah, the honest messenger and prophet, may God's peace and blessings be upon him, is an Arab from Quraysh (the tribe of the prophet), that God has chosen the Arab nation to serve as faith trustees charged with conveying His message which is contained in His Koran to all of mankind, and that the nation's role, accordingly, is a chosen role, that is, a leading role. And for the nation to maintain its leading role and to perform its responsibilities which God asked it to perform to keep the flame of the new heavenly faith, Islam, glowing, we have to maintain in a special unique way the required traits of faith within and without. The most important thing in Islam and all other heavenly faiths, after faith in the one God, is man's humanity and his capacity for cultivating land and working to establish justice there. Therefore, when a leader, president, or king within the Arab nation walks outside the confines of this path, when he fails to play his role toward the Arab individual, and when he fails to work to cultivate and maintain leadership traits within his personality to relay the message (of Islam) and establish justice on earth, he will not be forgiven by God even if he were to spend all his days and nights performing prayers and fasting.

How then would the situation be when the leader, the ruler fails to sing the praises of God, acts unjustly and ruthlessly, and disobeys God and shows arrogance? All Egyptians and all Arabs are well aware that the Arab states before the emergence of oil in the Arabs' lives as a major source of wealth and before the world's interest in it was as it is right now, had their own standing and ranks. They are aware that each state had its stature, that the position of Arab states, their influence, and their stature were the result of an accumulation of thousands of years of mental and physical work, diligence, and sacrifices.

All of us know that Arab countries have had nicknames and that these are the accumulation of long history and cultural associations. And so Egypt, the land of the Nile, had its stature and influence with the Arabs on the bases I have mentioned. Iraq, Mesopotamia and the rural land, had its stature and influence, as so with Arabia Felix

and Green Tunisia in addition to the Arabian Peninsula — the land
of Najd and Hejaz — and Bilad al-Sham. Even in Islam these had
their stature and role which was reinforced with faith and the honor
of carrying the Islamic message so that Egypt came to be known as
the land of the Kinana tribe, and the honor of al-Qadisiyya became
synonymous with the name of Iraq. This arrangement of place, role,
and influence was associated, as we pointed out, with the effort and
sacrifice of man and derives from a profound civilization that goes
far back in history.

Accordingly, no one felt aggrieved whenever the goals and the
general policies were common. Along with other factors, this
arrangement has played a positive role in the life of the nation and
its united stand. But, no sooner had the Arabs rid themselves of
Ottoman rule, hoping to be united as one nation, than oil was
discovered. And there came Europe's conspiratorial carve-up of the
Arab world, which was not limited to keeping the key (Arab)
countries away from the notion of grand unity, but fragmented
certain countries, including splitting Kuwait from southern Iraq.
European colonialism had made a point of keeping Arab territories
with oil deposits sparsely populated wherever possible so they would
remain too weak to resist colonial greed and shallow in terms of
culture and civilization. Indeed, colonialism was at pains to make
some of these countries mere distortions, having been severed from
the main body and the spirit of their tradition. Thus, oil-generated
wealth and the bulk of cultured and civilized Arabs have been kept
apart. And since the borders of these parts were drawn by
colonialism, and their rulers were installed by foreigners, they put
up barriers between themselves and other Arab countries and even
fostered the feeling among the people of their mini- states that, if
they were to conserve the sources of their wealth, they had to remain
aloof from the (Arab) nation and its causes. They opposed Arab
unity and the joint struggle, and the foreigner became their protector
and sponsor of their affluence. As happens with thieves, the ghost of
the theft of the wealth of the nation kept haunting the rulers of the
small parts with the result that they developed a terrible kind of
introspection to such an extent that there was a gap between their

words and consciences and it became impossible for anyone to know how to reassure them in order for them to be more responsive and how to keep their mischief at bay after they had been caught up with such feeling and became servants to foreigners. This particularly applies to the shaykhs of the Gulf oil, or most of them. The al-Sabah family were most prominent among them, since their theft was the more open and flagrant.

Iraq has for a long time suffered from them and from their conspiracies. Their anti-Iraq conspiracies became worse over the past few years. That is because they realized that Iraq rejected the policy of their masters, the colonizers; that it rejected the status of humiliation that they sought to impose on the Arabs; that it also refused to see Arab wealth used to damage the Arab's character, heritage, religion, and ethics; and that it sought to use this wealth to serve Arab goals and all people, considering it pan-Arab wealth.

At a time when all Arabs are bearing the burden signified by the existence of wealth in the Arab homeland, the benefits of this wealth must reach all Arabs. It should not remain in the hands of a tyrannical elite that uses it for licentiousness, corruption, and aggression. The aggression of the oil shaykhs used to increase against Iraq whenever the latter showed stronger adherence to the values of Arabism and Islam and also whenever it said...loud and clear that Jerusalem was Arab and that Palestine was Arab.

I can even say to you, Mr. President, and through you to the dear Egyptian people, that King Fahd's stand against Iraq and against Saddam Husayn is not because Kuwait has returned to its people after having been isolated in the quagmire of humiliation, filthy in the quagmire of corruption. Fahd and those who cooperated with him have begun to hatch plots against Iraq and Saddam Husayn after they became convinced that Iraq and Saddam Husayn were taking the side of the poor Arabs and not those living in the lap of luxury, who had forgotten God after forgetting the poor people, and that Iraq, Saddam Husayn, and his comrades would not abandon, under any circumstances, or under the weight of all conspiracies and intrigues, Palestine and holy Jerusalem. For these reasons and also because their masters and those with ill-gotten property were annoyed by, and rejected, the new Iraq and the policy being pursued by Saddam Husayn and his comrades, they then assumed a conspiratorial role for the same reason that they hated 'Abd-al-Nasir and conspired against him. They conspired against Saddam Husayn for additional reasons other than those that prompted them to conspire against 'Abd-al-Nasir.

Because God urges us to provide evidence so that those who are ready for persuasion can be persuaded, I enclose to you the transcript of a tape with Fahd's voice while conversing with an Arab ruler who was not a party with him to the conspiracy so that you can hear the tape and read the transcript. The conversation was held on 9 July 1990. God has enabled us to obtain this tape without any effort on our part. This tape will show you more and more why they are conspiring against Saddam Husyan. The main reason will be clear. It is because Saddam Husayn has rejected Israeli blackmail and threatened that he would reply to aggression. It is also because he is struggling through his leadership of the great Iraqi people for the return of Arab Palestine. You will see how Fahd even harbors malice toward 'Abd-al-Nasir who is in his tomb for the same reason. Furthermore, you will also see how he agrees with the Gulf oil countries to conspire, and how he asks them to procrastinate for two months until they can coordinate their positions and are able to harm Iraq even more.

Then, I assume your assuredness will be greater and you will arrive at the conviction that the Croesus of Kuwait and his like have been baneful germs eating away at all that is honorable and dear of the nation's possessions and all that provides the nation with spiritual or material power.

Also then, we will have added new evidence to the large amount that we possess to substantiate the argument that what has happened is the thing that should have happened and that the land of the Arabs, who are a single nation, will be inherited by the righteous slaves of God. If this is the case, then how should it be if this land were to be an Iraqi land that had become a base for conspiracy in order to cut off the breast of its mother and kill it after sucking its milk and blood?

Arab oil is for the Arabs; this is a slogan that we have raised since we were schoolboys and it is high time it was implemented to serve the Arabs and their values so that the Arabs can become what they should be, the vanguard of Muslims, by virtue of their faith, honor, morals, culture, and progress, and an example to be followed by the Islamic nation and by humanity as a whole.

Mr. President, you are the president of the Egyptian people — these dear people who endured a great deal because of oil. For, had it not been for oil, the price of Egyptian goods would not have risen as they have and the Egyptian people's clothing, food, houses, school, and cultural needs would not have become costlier. The purchasing power of the oil countries and their rulers has reflected negatively and dangerously on the life of our people and nation from the farthest point in the west to that in the east. In the past an Arab was not used to comparing lifestyles or looking up to the living standards of Westerners. However, the Egyptian young are now mingling with the young of the (United) Arab Emirates, Saudi Arabia, Kuwait formerly, and Qatar. When they learn about the latter's expenses and their lifestyles, the Egyptian young will start looking to a standard of living that is beyond their level and their purchasing power. This is because the one whom they want to emulate is an Arab like themselves and a student in their school. And the fathers of the Egyptian young might be better than the fathers of these by virtue of honor, work, culture, faith, and cleverness. When the Egyptian young, however, cherish certain aspirations and place their aspirations within a framework of comparison with these Arabs, they feel bitterness, they feel cheated.

Because their means do not allow them to have what they need, the Egyptian young might go astray while searching for means that will get for them what others have already got. This is one of the causes of social delinquency among men and women. In fact, such bitterness, and the feeling that the historical status of certain countries which once occupied a leading place has receded to be replaced by names that do not possess any qualifications except that they are oil states, has made the bitterness rise so much that it has reached rulers and leaders. Moreover, some of the aberrations of rulers in non-oil countries are caused by the bitterness over the unrighteous and the latter's slipping into things that bring them closer to a level they believe is the most efficient to maintain the degree of propriety befitting a ruler.

Arab women, as the popular saying goes, are the responsibility of the generous, and the same probably applies in the Egyptian countryside, especially in Upper Egypt. Therefore, preserving the honor of Egypt's girls and shielding them against corruption and being corrupted is your direct responsibility, Mr. President, just as it is my direct responsibility toward honorable Iraqi women. It is, indeed, a principled pan-Arab responsibility toward all whose rulers behave dissolutely. We cannot preserve the honor of the women of Egypt, Iraq, and other Arabs, nor will the hunger of the deprived in Egypt and elsewhere in the Arab world be satisfied or the door to social, economic, scientific, and cultural development in the Arab world open unless the right balance is restored between responsibility and influence, and unless Arab wealth is handled in a way that pleases God and is in accordance with His teachings.

Do you not know, Mr. President, that the personal wealth of the Croesus of Kuwait is $60 billion and that of King Fahd is $18 billion? I am quoting figures published in countries allied to these Croesuses. And yet the published figures may not tell the whole story. Do you not know, Mr. President, that reports published in the West claim that the so-called Kuwaiti Government has $220 billion invested and deposited in US and European banks? If their proceeds were to be invested in the Arab homeland it would become an ideal place. Do you not know, Mr. President, that US assistance to Egypt is a meager portion of the United States' profits from Arab wealth and that the share of Egypt's people in Arab wealth is far higher than this favor (*minna*) from the United States, on whose account you were pressured to send the army of the land of the Kinana tribe (Egypt) to face off the army of al-Qadisiyya (Iraq) and to give cover to the crime of criminal Americans as they occupy the land of the sanctities of Arabs and Muslims of Najd and Hejaz (Saudi Arabia)? Was it to advance such purposes that the Arab army of Egypt was founded? The people and army of Egypt are

Arab believers. They are, therefore, on the side of right against wrong. As their head of state, it is only right that you do not compliment, cover, or be involved in the crime. It is only right that you should take the side of the people of Egypt, the poor in Egypt, the Arab nation, and the poor of the Arab nation. It is only right that you should take the side of faith and be among the ranks of the faithful who are striving against the corrupt, the dissolute, the tyrants, and the army of invaders that has insulted the Ka'ba and the tomb of the messenger (Muhammad). Only then would the expression be appropriate to describe Arab nationalism and pan-Arabism and Islam and peace, as life is worthless under the yoke of injustice, occupation, invasion, and corruption, and denial of the spirit of the principles of Islam. Jihad is a right and an obligation. The faithful from the (Atlantic) Ocean to the (Arabian) Gulf are growing in number. The infidels, the hypocrites, and the invaders are trembling in anticipation of the major battle. God, His messenger, and the faithful are on our side, and if you should decide to be in this group you will win the approval of God and your people. Then you will be a dear brother, and God is great and let the lowly be accursed.

Source: FBIS-NES-90-165, 24 August 1990.

11. Saddam Husayn Repeats Call for Jihad
5 September 1990

Message from President Saddam Husayn to "the Iraqi people, faithful Arabs, and Muslims everywhere" on 5 September 1990 read by announcer. *Baghdad Domestic Service in A Rabic 1500 GMT, 5 Septermber 1990.*

In the name of God, the merciful, the compassionate. O great Iraqi people, O faithful Arabs wherever you may be, O Muslims in our Islamic world, wherever you recall your obligations to God as partners in the confrontation of right against falsehood and faith against evil. O sincere Islamists, for whatever path of faith in God and in human rights you have chosen and wherever you perform your duties before God, the great confrontation began on 2 August. Standing at one side of this confrontation are peoples and sincere leaders and rulers, and on the other are those who stole the rights of God and the tyrants who were renounced by God after they renounced all that was right, honorable, decent and solemn and strayed from the path of God until they eventually opposed it when they became obsessed by the devil from head to toe. It is the great confrontation of the age taking place in this part of the world, where the material has overwhelmed the spiritual and all moral and ethical values. Thus, there has been a disruption in the equation that God almighty wanted for humanity, which He conveyed through His books and messengers, whom He asked to convey specific duties to all mankind. Owing to the acts of the evildoers, man has been on the verge of losing even his humanity and being separated from the path of God or the path of God separated from him. It is the confrontation of right against falsehood, the confrontation of faith against infidelity, and a confrontation between the obligations to God almighty against the devil's tendency to appropriate the rights of humanity and misguide the ranks of the feeble.

Almighty God has made His choice, and the gathering of the faithful, militant, and mujahidin who dedicated themselves to principles have responded to His choice. Almighty God has chosen the Arab homeland as the field of confrontation and the Arabs as the leaders of the faithful gathering with the Iraqis as the vanguard force. Thus the message that God has wanted to convey since the first ray of faith emerged is being reaffirmed. This message is that the Arab homeland be the first arena of faith and that the Arabs be the permanent cadre to lead the faithful gathering on the path that pleases almighty God and that leads mankind to real happiness.

It is your turn, O Arabs, to save the entire human race, not only yourselves. Your turn has come to show your values and to highlight the meanings of the message of Islam in which you believe and which you practice. Your turn has come to save humanity from the injustice of the tyrants and usurpers who followed the path of inequity, corruption, dissolution, exploitation, arbitrariness, tyranny, and pride, led along the evil path by the United States of America. Your turn has come as a leading faithful cadre in the human gathering of believers to confront oppression and oppressors, and I do not believe you would relinquish this role to another.

Brothers, when the confrontation began, some thought that it was the outcome of a slogan raised in haste, and that to dissuade the gathering of the faithful from the path and its objectives, it was enough to accumulate a gathering of villains, reprobates, and infidels, and to accumulate the means of destruction on the border of the faithful, patient, and mujahid Iraq, so that the vanguard gathering would be defeated before all the faithful could build upon it. Their thinking and luck has failed them. This is because the kinsfolk of al-Qadisiyya* have chosen this path as a result of their deep belief in God and in the nation and its role. And, although they have depended on God in the confrontation, they have taken into consideration the worst that can be launched against them by the arrows of injustice and treachery. When they waged the

---

* A site in Iraq famous for the 637 battle in which the Arabs defeated the Persians.

confrontation, therefore, they did so with faithful hearts that do not know fear or suspicion and that only know the slogan of victory, and only victory, God willing. Ah, verily, the help of God is always near (Koranic verse).

O Arabs, you have proven to the inhabitants of the earth that when God chose you so that your nation would bear witness to the whole of humanity, He was right. Thus, have we made of you an *umma* (nation) justly balanced, that ye might be witness over the nations, and the apostle a witness over yourselves (Koranic verse).

The steadfast stone-throwing people who were assigned by God to perform the duty of showing right against the wrong of the Zionists led your ranks in showing great solidarity for Iraq, and in showing how capable right is, and how weak wrong becomes when it is confronted by right.

The manifestation of solidarity and demonstration of the disparity between right and wrong have followed: from Jordan, Yemen, Tunisia, Algeria, Libya, the Sudan, and Mauritania. The zeal of faith has exceeded the gathering of the faithful to extend to all the sons of the Arab nation and our Muslim world. And, after right was revealed wherever it was revealed correctly, the gathering of supporters extended to the wide expanse of humanity outside the realm of the Arab and Islamic world. Hence, the confrontation has acquired a comprehensive human character.

Brothers, the beginning of any confrontation of this kind always starts with a smaller number that includes only the household ("*Ahl al-Bayt,*" meaning the Prophet Muhammad's household). It will then transcend this household to humanity at large. In this confrontation, the household — with due respect to the rights of the Prophet Muhammad's household — is the (Islamic) nation which was chosen by God, so as to possess a leading faith among the gathering of the faithful. The gathering of the faithful does not presuppose an automatic sequence, but assumes intermingling of an Arab and a non-Arab on the basis of the ruling of the holy verse. Verily, the most honored of you in the sight of God is the most righteous of you.

Considering the circumstances of the confrontation in the time of the Prophet, the most vigorous opponents of the values of the (Islamic) message were among the ranks of the Arabs, led by those who have illegitimate interests, which could never stay where they are or the way they are, except at the expense of the humanity of man.

The evil gathering of those who have taken their side — those whom God has chosen that they not see the right path, having chosen wandering, evil, and corruption, led by those called by the foreigners the rulers of their peoples — are taking a stand against the faithful among the Arabs. But just as God has split the ranks of the infidel, so that people take the guided path from His true religion, He shall disrupt the misguided weak. Indeed, their gathering has been dispersed right from the beginning so that the upper hand will be for the deprived faithful who have known that the road to God is right, through their suffering against the gathering that has lost its path to God, when it degenerated into corruption and corrupted others and sought the help of infidels against faith and the faithful.

As for America's sea and air fleets, its armies and those who slipped with it into the abyss, they will only strengthen in us, the leadership, and the great people of Iraq, our faith in the path that we have chosen in order that God, the people, the nation, and humanity may bless us. The rattling of their weapons and the use of these weapons will only increase our determination to respond to sincere principles, their slogans and their applications, in social justice, in rejecting tyranny, division, and weakness. The motto of the faithful is: There is no going back; the believer will advance. This is our eternal motto which will not be dropped from our hands. Under the banner of faith and jihad, many heads will roll — heads that have never been filled with pride and whose owners never knew the path of faith. Let those who have been promised martyrdom have it.

Muslims everywhere, Fahd, Husni, and their allies from among those who have evil and base records have added to their injustice by repeating the role of Abu-Righal who acted as the guide of the Abyssinian Abraha (who led the attack on Ka'ba before Islam) on the road to pre-Islam Mecca, and was defeated by God with flights of birds and stones of baked clay.* Indeed, the part played by Abu-Righal was less vicious than their role when they called in invading armies that have occupied and desecrated the land housing the sacred places of Muslims and Arabs. Thus, we are duty-bound to engage in holy jihad so that we can liberate the two holy mosques from captivity and occupation, after the one who called himself their servant betrayed them. Your brothers in Iraq will know no peace of mind until the last soldier of occupation departs by choice or is expelled from the land of Arabism in Najd and Hejaz (Saudi Arabia).

We call on all Arabs to do what they can within their means in light of God's laws and the sanctities of jihad and struggle against this infidel and occupying presence to expose, without hesitation and through all means, the actions of traitors and their allies of corruption and oppression.

We appeal to the enduring and afflicted people of Hejaz; the oppressed people of Najd and the eastern province; the people of Mecca, al-Medina, Ha'il, Riyadh, and Jedda; the fraternal people in dear Egypt; and all the sons of our nation wherever they disagree with their rulers due to the differences over dignity, sovereignty, justice, and faith, to revolt against treason and traitors and against the infidel foreign occupation of the land of their shrines. We are with them. And more importantly, God is with them.

O brothers, the children of Iraq will prove, the children of Iraq who are deprived of milk will prove to those greedy invaders and their aides that they are more capable. Those who betrayed their nation, their honor as men, and the meanings and values of humanity will be vanquished before the steadfastness of children. The women of Iraq will prove to them that they are more accurate and skillful in managing things than those who lost the wisdom of management and accurate action. And even before all this, the men of Iraq are beyond comparison, this is because God and His angels are with the good and faithful people at a time when the evil people aligned

---

* *Hijara min sijjil,* the Arabic for stones of baked clay, was the name of the long-range missiles which Iraq hurled at Israel during the Gulf War.

themselves away from the path of good deeds, dignity, and honor. They went against all noble values. Wretched are their deeds.

Have you known, O brothers, in the history you have studied of someone who tried to starve a nation to death by preventing food from reaching them? Have you seen the acts of Nazism, which the West rants on about, claiming to hoist the banner of confrontation and comparing it to everything loathsome and inhuman..., to it, cut off medicine from a whole nation so that the sick will die because there is no medicine? Have you ever seen in the history you have read children dying because of an intentional decision to stop milk from reaching them? If you have not seen or heard about this before, the United States had done all this, urged by Zionism. In doing so, it has been supported by some Western politicians who have been offered a position of rank or have been pushed toward a position of rank by the advertisements of Zionist propaganda and financial institutions; those who have trampled...humanitarian principles underfoot, thus adding themselves to the list of those who will be cursed by history.

The Arab and Iraqi nation will not forget their evil deed; they will be backed by the gathering of humanity alongside the gathering of the faithful Muslims, after humanity awakens from its sleep and reveals justice in its true form.

The children of Iraq, before the people of Iraq, do not want us to beg for the milk they need from the infidels and shameless. Their valiant fathers and the glorious daughters of al-Qadisiya will extract life for them relying on God. We will see the portraits of the children who defeated the tyrants and the superpower etched in the hearts of all those who will be liberated and released by this confrontation after the forces of the tyrants retreat and their abortive gathering flees.

History will record immortal pages on those men and women who stand as one against the invaders who desecrated with their soldiers' feet the land of Najd and Hejaz. God will not champion the believers over the infidels unless the believers show that they are well prepared for the confrontation and the sacrifices.

O brothers, your Iraqi brothers have chosen a vanguard position in your group. In light of their long experience, they know that the preparation for sacrifice of those who chose the vanguard position should be in harmony with the position chosen. They know that to God their position in such a choice will be in harmony with the scope of their endurance, patience, and sacrifices. They believe in God and the duty called for by God. They will remain as they have always been — they will make a mockery of the unjust blockade and will not attach any weight other than the weight of evil. They will pray to their mother, the land of Iraq, which will respond with its bounty which it never withheld from its sons. It has always been the supporter of the fighters in every defeat they inflicted on the invaders throughout history. They will be able to defeat the camp of invaders, whether it remains the same or is doubled with the dispatch of other troops.

O Iraqis, and O you brothers everywhere, such a group or a larger group is appropriate for the seriousness with which you have prepared for the confrontation. The believers should not confront a group similar to their own or slightly greater.

Apostle, rouse the believers to the fight. If there are 20 amongst you, patient and persevering, they will vanquish 200; if a hundred, they will vanquish a thousand of the unbelievers, for those are a people without understanding (Koranic verse).

What then will the situation be if we know that the number of Iraqi volunteers who came to sacrifice their lives for principles and the homeland exceeds 5 million Iraqis, not to mention the proud men within the ranks of the armed forces who total more than 1 million combatants? For the invaders to attack this number, they have to mass twice this number. Consequently, the invaders need to mass a minimum of 12 million combatants. O brothers, you know that the air force cannot settle a ground battle, regardless of the sophisticated weaponry. This is the rule governing all conventional and liberation wars. The Vietnamese people were the last to confront this sophisticated capability.

In spite of the fact that the Americans turned what was then South Vietnam into a real base for serving their military operations against what was then North Vietnam and secured there all that would offer their troops comfort and entertainment, these opportunities do not exist — or are not as abundant — on the holy lands of Najd and Hejaz. Their outcome (in Vietnam) is known to you. How would they do then if they were to confront Iraq under completely different circumstances, except for what the people, including the Vietnamese and Iraqi people, have in common: the determination to face the invaders?

Iraq's support at present is all for the honorable leaders and rulers, the Arab nation's people, all the well-meaning and faithful sons of the Islamic nation, the well-intentioned throughout the world led by the oppressed people who are treated unfairly because of the injustice inflicted by the exploiting Americans and others. First and foremost, God is with them.

Those involved will be sorry, and their gathering will be utterly routed if they undertake a military confrontation. Their footprints will be erased from the entire region, and then Jerusalem will be restored, free and Arab, to the lap of faith and the faithful. Palestine will be liberated from the Zionist invaders and the Arab and Islamic nation will see a sun that will never set. They will be in God's protection when they have returned to the Almighty. God is great, God is great, God is great. Accursed be the lowly ones.

(Signed) Saddam Husayn
(Dated) 15 Safar 1411 Hegira, corresponding to 5 September 1990 A.D.

Source: FBIS-NES-90-173, 6 September 1990.

12. Saddam Husayn Addresses Message to Bush and Gorbachev 8 September 1990

Text of Iraqi President Saddam Husayn's message to US President George Bush and Soviet President Mikhail Gorbachev on the eve of the Helsinki summit. *Baghdad INA in Arabic 1701 GMT, 8 September 1990.*

In the name of God, the merciful, the compassionate. From Saddam Husayn to Presidents Mikhail Gorbachev and George Bush. Peace be upon you. You will meet tomorrow on 9 September 1990, corresponding to 19 Safar 1411 Hegira. Your meeting will be watched with keen and unusual interest by the whole world, including the peoples of a region which God blessed by making us a part of the Arab nation, which was honored by God as the cradle of prophets and messages throughout time.

While you will be in a position to make decisions that affect humanity, for better or worse, you will be flanked by angels on one side and devils on the other, each arguing his case according to his own instincts and God's will, and God shall prevail over all.

I am neither telling nor requesting either of you to make this or that decision, since each of you has a will of his own and is free to make his own decision, aided by the intellect provided by God, or according to the will of God and the dictates of His conscience.

But, after relying on God the omnipotent and almighty, I would say this: Before you make whatever decisions you will, I would like to begin by saying:

1. That Iraq has not invaded any of your countries, and has never had any premeditated intention to cause harm to anyone at all, or any country, or legitimate interests. Iraq is a peace-loving nation. We desire peace which is based on justice. Iraq respects the free choices of others, so as to satisfy God and the people. The Iraqi people and leadership rely on the one and only God, and conduct

themselves in a manner according to His guidance so as to win the approval of God — this being an inevitable option to promote the requirements of their patriotism and the honor of their pan-Arab and human affiliations, and the requirements of the well-being and happiness of the people of Iraq, to whom God decreed rights which He decided to spell out in books to all humanity through His prophets.

He who believes in God must have principles and values in his mind. And when these become clear and are borne in mind, they are certain to keep man — who is naturally bent toward evil and harm — from taking the path of evil and harm, and will guide him on the road of faith and forgiveness.

2. More than 1,400 years ago, enticed by the devil and intoxicated by his power to expand and dominate, Abraha the Abyssinian had sought to occupy the Ka'ba, whose land is now occupied by US forces and by those who have been tempted to do evil. Angered by this attempt, God trounced...him, and so Abraha returned with a bowed head and lowered banners. He did not dare ever to attack the Ka'ba again. God, who smashed the armies of Abraha, which had been tempted to trespass on this holy land more than 1,400 years back, is immortal. Those who have trespassed on the House of God and the tomb of the messenger of God had better take heed and remember the time-honored saying: The House has a God to protect it. Everyone should remember that the Ka'ba is the direction to which 1 billion Muslims turn in prayer, five times a day. "From wherever thou starest forth, turn of the sacred mosque" (part of Koranic verse).

It is the place to which Muslims make their annual pilgrimage. The humiliation to this place and to the tomb of the Prophet Muhammad — may God's peace be upon him — through the occupation and invasion, is not only directed against 200 million Arabs whom God honored as permanent angels to communicate the concepts of the message, but also against 1 billion Muslims. Whatever pretexts and excuses are advanced by transgressors, God shall not forgive them, and His virtuous slaves will rise up and resist this dissolute action with all their might. God shall bring victory to

those who rally to His cause, and the unjust shall be defeated.
3. Before either of you make a decision on Kuwait, you should both remember that the Arab nation is one nation, even though it was fragmented as it is now; that this is a fact that cannot be denied by its rulers, leaders, peoples, or sons; that the sweeping majority of its sons, rulers, and peoples are honored to be part of this great nation; and that they are longing to be one political entity, regardless of the specific characteristics of this or that country. Besides, the slogan of struggling to achieve the nation's unity in an effective political entity is being translated into acts in broad daylight to show and serve the human aspects of the sons of the single Arab nation and also to serve all of mankind. This slogan was upheld by the Arabs a long time before any of our generation reached power, and also before the sons of younger generations were born. Making sacrifices to achieve this is an honor and duty cherished by all the sincere and faithful, who believe that they will be honored if they do not forget it or do not fail to struggle to achieve it.

Kuwait has been part of Iraq in the not-so-remote past. The Kuwaiti people are part of the Iraqi people. The British colonial powers separated it from Iraq for colonial reasons and purposes. Iraq did not recognize this measure even in 1958, when Nuri al-Sa'id, the friend of the West and Britain which made this hateful colonial decision, was prime minister of Iraq. Furthermore, 'Abd al-Karim Qasim, a pro-USSR prime minister of Iraq (title as heard), made the same decision in 1961 which we have made. Despite the fact that Nuri al-Sa'id, who was a pro-Western prime minister of Iraq in 1958, and 'Abd al-Karim Qasim, who was the pro-USSR prime minister of Iraq in 1961, either annexed Kuwait or claimed it on this basis — considering it part of Iraq — those who are opposing us nowadays did not oppose them at that time, despite the fact that the current situation provides more reasons for the adoption of this decision. That is because the backward, corrupt former Kuwaiti rulers conspired against Iraq and their greater people when they were about to dash Iraq into a deep abyss. Anyone who wants to obtain further details on this issue can read the enclosed file (not further specified).

The attempts by some people to restore things to what they were before 2 August 1990 are impractical and futile attempts. Additionally, they are attempts aiming at promoting the instability of the region. They even constitute a premeditated conspiracy against the Arab nation at the head of which is lofty Iraq.

On the basis of these facts, and regardless of the convergence or divergence of views between this or that son of the Arab homeland or among foreigners, duty dictates at this phase that you recall these facts, that you know for sure that what we are telling you right now concerns facts of the Arab homeland and nation, and that this is not an invention or a mere excuse to justify or cover up controversial purposes.

When you consider these facts in their proper perspective and show humility once you know the rights of mankind, you will realize that the Arabs, by their recollection of the relevant background on the basis of these facts, are more capable than others of resolving all inter-Arab affairs. You will also then realize that foreigners, including yourselves, are incapable of offering the proper solution to an Arab issue whose parties are Arabs, in the way that the Arabs could, even if we were to rule out any premeditated intentions of either of you. We are sure — and let God and history be our witness — that foreign intervention will complicate matters and fail to offer a solution.

4. If discussion of this issue leads you to believe that you are the guardians of the international organization's resolutions, you must remember that the international organization has, ever since its formation, taken many other resolutions before taking the resolutions pertaining to Iraq. Some of these resolutions pertain to Arab causes, some of whose parties are Arab and others foreign. Foremost of these issues is the question of the persevering and afflicted people of Palestine, and the people of the Golan Heights, despite the fact that these resolutions were taken at a time when there was a kind of balance of power between the international superpowers and big powers. The situation we were in then is not at all similar to the situation now. The UN Security Council has never adopted such hasty and emotional resolutions, and its resolutions

have never been on this level of harshness and injustice, which reveals that there is a premeditated objective behind them.

Whoever needs to be reminded of the rabid campaign that preceded the events of 2 August led by the heads of the US and Zionist organizations — that unjust campaign against Iraq — will surely realize the type of objective concealed in the emotional campaign within the Security Council orchestrated by the United States which proceeded to unilaterally adopt more unjust resolutions against Iraq by implementing them in its own special method of siege tactics.

5. Perhaps what will emerge before you in your discussions when you meet is merely the Iraq whose population does not exceed 18 million, and which is a Third World country separated from you by two worlds of development, and that you belong to the first world, which is superior in the civil and military fields. If this is what emerges before you, it will urge you to take resolutions which will give you back a part of your sense of responsibility to avert the evils of war and its tragedies from the region. Good lies in what God chooses and I pray that the Merciful will fill hardened hearts with the light of belief in pursuing the just, good, and humanitarian path of their behavior — especially Bush's heart. If you view the situation and view Iraq from this point of view just to make it easier for those who think that they can commit aggression, then humanitarian duty and ethical responsibility makes me duty bound to highlight the perils of such thinking — especially if these facts encourage anyone harboring evil thoughts to facilitate a strike on the people of Iraq in the hope of realizing his evil and aggressive desires.

The people of Iraq, O masters of the White House and the Kremlin, are the people who had the honor to show humanity the right path to its humanity when they taught it the alphabet and writing 6,000 years ago, and when they taught it law 4,500 years ago. It was the country that taught humanity so much of what it had not known. Iraq is also part of the glorious Arab nation, which God honored when He chose His prophets and messengers from among its sons and when He chose its land as the birthplace of all heavenly messages and books. Iraq is also part of a nation of 200 million souls that extends from the Atlantic Ocean to the Arabian Gulf.

Based on the fact that the Arab nation is one nation, the Iraqi people will stand united against injustice and the unjust, and against the invasion and the invaders. The traitors, who encouraged those who have been deluded, will be a small minority. When the battle has taken place, then the Iraqi people, whom God has chosen to be in the forefront, will triumph, the Arab nation's forces will triumph, and all the invaders will be defeated. The aggressors' banner will be torn apart, and they will be deafened by the shouts of "God is great and damned be the invaders." God almighty's power will be the guide to all believers, and He will not let down the nation which He honored to carry the message. In any case, the billion Muslims will be the depth of the faithful masses, with which the slaves of God, who know that we are right and the invaders are wrong, will support and be in harmony with. Then, it will be useless to bite one's fingernails.

The position taken by each of you, Presidents Mikhail Gorbachev and George Bush, and the decisions that either of you reach in this meeting of yours will determine the position of each of your countries and the weight they attach to humanity. It may even determine a principal part of their destinies in the long run. I am certain that he who deviates in thought and action from the right course will bring his country down one or more degrees in the scale of what is recorded for and against it, and in the scale of its status.

He who represents the Soviet Union must remember that worries and suspicions about the superpower status assumed by the Soviet Union have been crossing the minds of all politicians in the world for some time, especially after the United States has begun to act singlehandedly in the world and to behave arrogantly without having the party that used to be there in the past to guide it to the more balanced path to follow. Those concerned must choose this critical time and this critical case to restore to the Soviet Union its status through adopting a position that is in harmony with all that is just and fair, and to reject the discriminatory approach which the United States of America is following to keep its distance from the just solution to all cases of the region in accordance with the basis mentioned in our initiative of 12 August 1990.

President Bush must not bring his country and its status down to a lower level, because we are certain that its position will drop on the scale of appreciation and effectiveness if it falls into the abyss of war, and if its armies and the armies of its allies remain on the land of our sanctuaries, and if the unjust blockade, which is denying the Iraqi people even their food and medicine and the children of Iraq the milk they need, remains in force. God will be against the aggressors, the heads of traitors will roll, and God is great.

(Signed) The believing slave of God, Saddam Husayn
(dated) 18 Safar 1411 Hegira, corresponding to 8 September 1990

Source: FBIS-NES-90-175, 10 September 1990.

13. Saddam Husayn's Initiative Offers Free Oil to Third World
10 September 1990

Statement by President Saddam Husayn issued on 10 September 1990 — read by announcer. *Baghdad Television Service in Arabic 1503 GMT, 10 September 1990.*

In the name of God, the merciful, the compassionate. Brothers and friends, esteemed leaders and peoples of the Third World countries, peace be upon you.

In describing you and us as the Third World, the big and developed countries wanted to describe not the gap that exists between us and them in scientific, technical, and economic

development and the degree of these kinds of development in general
— for which the colonialist system, which constituted the basis of
the developing countries' world, was primarily responsible — but
wanted in describing our world as the Third World, to define the
human level which they decided to give us in their dealings with us
and their views of us.

This has been their actual behavior and dealing with all.
Therefore, brothers, do not be surprised when the big and developed
countries do not accord a degree of attention to your issues,
problems, and humanity in every measure they take or decision they
make. On this basis also, those who decided to invade the oil
countries in the Middle East and insulted the sanctities of the
Muslims when they occupied the land of Najd and Hejaz did not ask
nor answer the question of what harm will befall the Third World
countries as a result of their shameful action.

At a time when oil monopolies began making illegal profits as a
result of this crisis, they left the Third World states to wallow in their
crises because of the increase in the oil prices resulting from their
crime — an increase the economy of the Third World cannot
absorb. If there is less oil, we have absolutely no doubt that you will
only receive quantities of oil that are in excess of the need of the big
and more developed countries, even if you suffer big disasters.

On the basis of this assessment and the spirit of brotherhood and
the solidarity of us and our Arab nation, which is part of your state
and fate, we have been targeted by the United States, Zionism, and
their satellite imperialist states. On the basis of this situation also,
we have maintained solidarity with you in all previous circumstances
and conditions. We have called for easing your burden at the
non-aligned conference in Havana in 1979. Iraq at the time was
faithful to its call when it conceded the differences in the oil price
increase to the Third World states which had bought oil from it. The
states affected by this decision must still remember this gracious
initiative.

Out of this appreciation and feeling of brotherhood and solidarity
with you and in appreciation for your just position toward the
fateful Arab issues, led by the issue of Palestine, we today declare

that we are your brothers and that we and you have the same fate. Therefore, we now declare our readiness to supply the needy Third World countries with Iraqi oil free of charge. Those who wish to take advantage of these arrangements, which we assume are not covered by the US boycott as they do not involve buying and selling — we say, those who wish that, must submit their applications to us, indicating the quantity and type of oil they need. If we are unable to transport the oil to them in our tankers, they must arrange for it at their own expense.

Brothers, this decision has been made on a principled and moral basis to ease your burden and to maintain solidarity with you at a time when we are able to fulfill such a role. This position has not and will not be linked to the kind of decision you make and to your position on the current crisis because we respect the views of states and peoples and know that each one has its own considerations and positions. We do not presuppose identity in all issues for the maintenance of ties of friendship and brotherhood. We also do not get angry as a result of differences in positions on the basis of different views and differences in facts and information. We only get angry when any imperialist state tries to impose its position on us by force as an expression of the complex of their lack of respect for the Third World countries and peoples and their failure to treat them with human equality and appreciation.

Our greetings to you and to all the oppressed and poor peoples. May God's peace and blessings be upon you. God is witness to our intentions.

(Signed) Your brother, Saddam Husayn
(Dated) 20 Safar 1411 Hegira, corresponding to 10 September 1990.

Source: FBIS-NES-90-177, 12 September 1990.

14. Saddam Husayn Calls for Release of All Foreigners
6 December 1990

Text of President Saddam Husayn's message to the National Assembly speaker and members on 6 December 1990 — read by announcer. *Baghdad Domestic Service in Arabic 1138 GMT, 6 December 1990.*

In the name of God, the merciful, the compassionate. Mr. National Assembly Speaker, members, peace be upon you. Under difficult conditions, the strength of the believers' affiliation and loyalty is put to the test. Their action in the service of principles is also put to the test. Iraqis in general, and you amongst them, have proved that on very dark nights the spark of faith glows in a much nicer way than on ordinary nights. Adherence to the supreme principles governing the relation between man and his creator and his duty toward Him, as well as the relation between the Iraqis with all peoples, becomes even stronger in the more difficult circumstances.

And, just as the continued endeavor is required on earth, the correct answers to the continuous test are also required, without making the test or success in it dependent on a certain phase and time.

On the basis of these principles and what we desire — that the influence of the believers expands, and that the knowledge of mankind in general expands with the believers' principles and the truth of their mission — we believe that, this time, the National Assembly is asked to take a decisive and final decision concerning a humanitarian issue, which you, and the whole world, know about.

National Assembly members, the thing that most worries the faithful mujahid (struggler), the honorable struggler, and the brave fighter — who has the values of the chivalrous believer — is when the trenches in the battle arena get mixed and when some people — who do not want to fight and who are not among the evildoers — get trapped in the space between the two trenches. This worry becomes deep grief when those kinds of people are harmed because of the level and type of the conflict.

The foreigners who were prevented from traveling are among those people in the battle between right, led by Iraq's great people and valiant armed forces, and evil, whose failing mass is led by Bush, the enemy of God. As you and my brothers in the leadership know, I realize that, despite what they had to put up with, denying those people the freedom to travel has rendered a great service to the cause of peace. And, because God has taught us that forbidden things should never be resorted to except in very urgent cases and without any excesses, we must not keep these emergency measures, especially this measure, any longer.

The days, weeks, and months through which our people and nation have passed have been such that our options, even those concerning the nature and form of defense, were not open or without limits in every area and all conditions. For instance, our valiant forces did not have the chance to complete their concentrations in order to confront the possibilities of military aggression against them in the Kuwaiti governorate. So, any measure that was taken to delay the war may not have been correct from the humanitarian and practical standpoints and under established norms, but it has provided an opportunity for us to prepare for any eventuality.

We have now reached the time when, with God's care, our blessed force has become fully prepared, if God wills that we should fight in defense of His values and ideals against the infidels, profligates, and traitors, and also in defense of the great national, pan-Arab, and humanitarian gains.

Gentlemen, good people — men and women of different nationalities and political trends — have come to Iraq. Dear brothers from Jordan, Yemen, Palestine, Sudan, and the Arab Maghreb have also consulted with us on this issue, as on others. We have felt, guided by our humanitarian feelings, that the time has come to make a firm decision on this subject. We had considered a timing different from the present one; namely, the occasion of Christmas and New Year, which are of special significance to Christians in the world, including Christians in the West.

However, the appeal by some brothers, the decision of the Democratic majority in the US Senate, and the European Parliament's invitation to our foreign minister for dialogue — all these have encouraged us to respond to these good, positive changes, changes that will have a major impact on world public opinion in general, and US public opinion in particular, in restraining the evil ones who are seeking and pushing for war as the option they have chosen out of their evil tendencies and premeditated intentions to do harm.

In view of all this, we have found that the exigencies that permitted the impermissible, and thus prevented the travel of foreigners, have weakened and have been replaced by something stronger — namely, this positive change in public opinion, including the change in US public opinion, which will constitute a restraint on the intentions and decisions of the evil ones, who are led in their evil intentions and steps by the enemy of God, Bush.

Therefore, I call on you, brothers, to make your just decision and allow all foreigners on whom restrictions were placed to enjoy the freedom of travel and to lift these restrictions, with our apologies for any harm done to any one of them. God, the almighty, grants forgiveness.

Brothers, I ask you, and through you I ask the Iraqi people and our brave armed forces, to maintain your alertness and vigil because the armies of aggression are still on our holy lands, in the Arabian Peninsula, and the evil ones are talking of war. Bush's invitation for talks, as far as we can discern, has continued to bear the possibilities of their inclination toward aggression and war. The buildup is growing.

Therefore, the steadfast believers, both on the level of the public and on the level of our armed forces, should not fall in the trap in which some have fallen in the past.

May God protect you and protect our people and nation, steer humanity from what God hates, help the faithful to carry out what God wishes, and smite the infidels and traitors after exposing them and their shameful deeds. He is the best supporter and backer. God is great, accursed be the infidels and traitors, who gave the oppressors and infidels the opportunity to invade the holy land. Glory and greatness to the mujahidin of the occupied land and all the steadfast mujahidin and fighters of our great Arab nation.

(Signed) Saddam Husayn
(dated) Thursday, 18 Jumada al-Ula, 1411 of the Hegira, corresponding to 6 December 1990

Source: FBIS-NES-90-235, 6 December 1990.

15. Saddam Husayn Speaks on Army Day
6 January 1991

Speech by President Saddam Husayn on the 70th anniversary of the establishment of the Iraqi Army on 6 January 1991 — live or recorded. *Baghdad Domestic Service in Arabic 0805 GMT, 6 January 1991.*

In the name of God, the merciful, the compassionate. May we hurl the truth against falsehood, and it knocks out its brain, and behold falsehood doth perish (Koranic verse).

O great Iraqi people, O brave men in our valiant armed forces, O honest faithful men in the nation, who are looking toward every inherited glory and pride sponsored and accepted by God, this day, 6 January every year, marks the anniversary of the army of people, your army in great Iraq. On this day, we take time to think about the past and our hopes. And hope expands to cover all the present and future, and to reach all the meanings of pride, sovereignty, liberation, and victory that please God and further the believers' distinguished position in today's world, on whose land the scorpions and vipers of treason and injustice spread like the swordfishes of treason and depravity, and the mean sharks prevail in it and on its seas and oceans *vis-à-vis* any possible opportunity.

When we contemplate 6 January this year, this day is unique as it is a day for the army, people, and nation. In fact, I say without any hesitation it is a day for humanity; its human characteristics and repercussions will appear to people, historians, and researchers in accordance with this description and aspiration for the future when its days become part of a glorious past, God willing, as it is the reality of this great mujahid (struggling) army.

Thus, it appears to you how, in certain historical circumstances, situations, and stages, all the glorious days — or many of those days — are represented in one single day; that is, it is sufficient to point at one day so that all the meanings and the brightness of light and pride will appear. And on the other hand, the longest stages and the large number of days cannot represent one single day in other circumstances.

The day which carries the weight of days in terms of great meanings in a basic side of the march of pride is 6 January. It is a day in the history of the jihad of the people of Iraq and the jihad of the nation, the history of their valiant army, our army and the brave armed forces in Iraq, whom we honor today and celebrate their great day. This day has become the day of all the glorious days of the Arabs in this stage. This day represents and also carries the slogans of shining glory, the struggler of our kinfolk and people, the heroes of stones in dear Palestine. It is a commemoration and symbol of all their sacrifices, their struggle, and jihad and the only gate for their aspiration and hope for pride, liberation, glory, and for a life in which people would live without humiliation or privation as long as the army and the armed Forces remain a living and honest part in a march with this description, and with these objectives and aspirations, which inspire them in their march forward.

These are the traits of our army and armed forces, and this is their eternal pledge before the people and the nation, God willing. It is the good luck of this army that it has begun to achieve its objectives and fight its enemies on the borders of the homeland, depending on the depth and ability to mass troops and rally resources in terms of strategies and operations secured by the homeland and its sons. At the same time, the objectives of the confrontation are not viewed as only national or pan-Arab accomplishments.

They go beyond this to assume their proper description and to see their meanings go beyond the nation and the country as well as their just causes to the realm of mankind, showing duties and effects that have something to do with the depth of the nation's cultural and human role and that harmonize and interact with all the spiritual laws God enacted for the nation so that it should observe them in its life and in its relationship with the Lord of the Heavens and the Earth. God made the nation a witness to all mankind, while He made the Prophet Muhammad, the messenger of God, may God's peace be upon him, a witness to it.

What a great honor it is for you, O comrades within our armed forces; O comrades in arms who cherish the principles whose meanings were vindicated and whose translation into acts and deeds were based on this description of the victorious march, God willing! What a great honor it is for everybody wearing khaki and bearing the arms of the faithful to perform these duties, displaying the honor of the faithful soldier and Arab soldiership of which we read and heard when we were students in school — the honor of the army of the faith, liberation, and conquest in the early stages of the Islamic mission, the army of Muhammad Bin 'Abdallah, the Prophet of God, sent to all mankind, and the army of the well-guided caliphs. We had hopes and we had in our imagination clear and conspicuous images of all this without seeing examples of it on the ground. We found in the examples of struggle and jihad on Arab lands demonstrated by the proud and faithful men and the patient and faithful women who epitomized the community of Muhammad Bin 'Abdallah and the roles of prophets and messengers in their Arab societies over many long years what comforted the hearts, allowed for hope to remain vivid, and ensured that endeavors will remain serious and persistent. Thus, they, within their own hearts, lived in this good way in which they demonstrated faith in God and in the role of the nation, after a firm faith and an unlimited ability to give to nurture a struggle and a jihad that cannot be stopped by difficulties and sacrifices, had made its dwelling within their minds and chests. Thus, the mujahidin, preceded by martyrs, became, as they are nowadays, the flagpole of this struggle and jihad along the long path which allowed for the accomplishment of the objectives that have been accomplished. Some objectives are yet to be attained. However, over all this past period and until recently, the army of the faith for which we waited and which we wanted was not founded. This continued until the nation's army was established in the great Iraq of faith, sacrifices, and glorious giving embodying meanings of struggle and jihad.

What a great honor it is for us, O brothers, O comrades-in-arms, to become part of this march, which is bordering on, and in fact dealing with, glory in all of its meanings on the ground, and enjoying the satisfaction of the nation's sons as illustrated by their sincere feelings and powerful cooperation. In fact, and this is more important, this march should also enjoy God's satisfaction as it has established this great bridge that links the meanings sought by our march and the brave Iraqi armed forces and the meanings once sought by the march of Muslims and the army of Muslim mujahidin in early Islam through dignity based on deep faith in the historical significance of Medina, Damascus, Baghdad, and Andalusia.

What a great honor it is for you to achieve several aims in one battle, even if such a battle is as complicated as the crucial battle. You are in one battle. You have been afforded a historic opportunity that your deceased fathers and forefathers awaited for a long time without seeing it with their own eyes; namely, the return of the branch to the origin; the return of Kuwait or the (*umm al-nida*) (mother of the call) to the origin, great Iraq, to become truly, and not just a claim or wishful thinking, the 19th governorate on the beloved map of Iraq to create a strong political Iraq for the present and the future as a living part of the camp of the faithful and as a model for the nation in its modern age and on the path of its struggle for unity.

In the same battle, and just as Palestine has been and still is the symbol of all Arab strugglers and the banner of the jihad for all mujahidin among the sons of the nation, you and the heroes of the stones have turned the slogans on the path of struggle for the liberation of Palestine into a legitimacy acknowledged not only by the sons of the Arab nation, but by all righteous men and all the faithful in the world. You and the stone-throwing children have made the possibility of liberation and expulsion of invaders both visible and tangible, and this dream will soon come true, God willing, so it will be seen by the eyes that have been afflicted by trachoma and strained by the mirages created by rulers and politicians who have abandoned God and insistence on justice. Thus, mercy, honor, hope, and victory have also abandoned them.

In the same battle, you, the people, and nation are fighting against social and economic injustice and the unfair discrimination that have afflicted the nation as a result of disobedience and the actions of the disobedient who hold Arab nationality, or as a result of foreign injustice. You are waging a battle against double standards, injustice, corruption, and decadence whether on the level of the nation and the Arab homeland or on the level of mankind and the world at large.

The battle you are waging today is, therefore, the crucial battle for all of these reasons. It is the battle that God almighty has willed and that has enabled you, through His divine choice, to be in the lead of those who will win its reward from God, and those who will win its honor, in proportion to the role and sacrifices entailed. The results — with what we have at hand and what God wants, and what we are still hoping for — will be great. The whole world and all the coming generations will speak about your stage and your battle in the way they deserve. And the positive effects will prevail and will be felt throughout the world and by all humanity.

After what we have said, is the saying that it is God's will not that of truthful Muslims and experienced rulers? It is indeed a true saying. It is the will of God almighty; the will of man in it is merely an obedient and yet a choosing will. It is obedient to what God wants and accepts; however, it chooses the arena and objectives of virtue, dignity, and faith, and the role of Muslims in life and their role against injustice and the unjust, corruption and the corrupt, and against the devil of the age — that is, the stupid US Administration and its protégé, the Zionist entity, and those cursed ones who allied themselves with it on evil and vice and tyranny. Let there arise out of you a band of people inviting to all that is good, enjoining what is right and forbidding what is wrong. They are the ones to attain felicity (Koranic verses). Consider also what the Prophet said: "Whoever sees an iniquitous action should change it by his hand; if he cannot, by his tongue; if he cannot, then by his heart, and that is the least that the faithful can do."

Brothers, comrades in arms and in faith, a battle thus described — considering its character, reward, honor, and effects — entails a sacrifice proportionate in quantity and quality, considering also its tangible and intangible results which please the friend and anger the enemy. Above all, and more importantly, are its results which will please God and the great forefathers while in their last abode.

Because the sacrifices and the conceivable difficulties, in addition to the difficulties that have already become tangible and visible, are among the things that can be understood and accepted insofar as they are willed by God and the mujahidin's choice of the road of jihad and virtue leading to them, we are speaking today about an aspect that might not have drawn the attention of everyone at the same level of seriousness; that is, the direct answer to a specific question. If the difficulties and sacrifices in the crucial battle are conceivable, then what are the facilities that have been provided by the crucial battle so as to facilitate the jihad of the mujahidin at the level of the nation and the level of Iraq and its armed forces?

You may know, brethren, that the achievement of all national, pan-Arab, and humanitarian aims combined will require the same sacrifices as those devoted to achieving these aims separately. This combination will produce a jihad and struggling momentum and unlimited conviction and faith. You know that if these national, pan-Arab, and humanitarian aims were separate and if the nation, people, and armed forces were to wage consecutive battles, the crucial battle might not take longer than any of these separate battles and would not have required more sacrifices as we have said. It is inconceivable that the battle for Palestine and the liberation of Palestine will be short if it is meant to be serious and glorious, nor is it conceivable that its sacrifices will be simple. The battle against the tyranny represented by the US Administration and the slogans of oppression, which it raises on the international and regional levels, and expelling the forces of infidelity and infidels from the sanctities of the Muslims, cannot be short. No serious accomplishments can be achieved in this battle without serious sacrifices. This applies to resisting double standards, injustice, corruption, social degeneration, hegemony, and economic injustice on the level of the world and the region. Of course, no one should be led into believing that the battle for the unity of new Iraq following the great call which liberated Kuwait from the injustice of the oppressors and corrupt ones in the al-Sabah family will be a short battle whose sacrifices are simple.

According to this description of the battle, and under these circumstances, whose characteristics and complications are known on both the pan-Arab and humanitarian levels as well as the level of Iraq and the rest of the Arab countries, it is natural for us to say that if the battle is divided into arenas, issues, slogans, and aims, it might split efforts and fighters and enable the opposite sides — once the faithful gathering is split up according to the priorities of its national, pan-Arab, and humanitarian interests — to alienate ranks from a unified concentration on issues according to their correct priorities. These sides might at subsequent stages spread chaos that splits ranks on the basis of wondering about the time, sacrifice, and required effort each separate battle deserves.

The opposite ranks can also obstruct the timing or neutralize for some time the subsequent action of the subsequent battles after absorbing the surprise of the first battle, weakening the reasons of distinction or superiority in it, and using the negative aspects of the separate battle in their favor in subsequent battles.

Waging a comprehensive battle for the sake of all the objectives of our nation and our people in a single effort is a correct situation in all ideological and practical aspects. The facilities that are being presented and that have been really presented by the crucial battle on the regional, pan-Arab, and human levels as well as on the level of the faithful gathering — so that their ranks will further close and so that the belief of the believers will be stronger in the soundness of the slogans and policies and the expansion of the theater of operations to include the whole nation and all the good believers — are serious and cannot be presented at all by a battle that is not comprehensive.

At the same time, there are technical facilities of a tactical, strategic, and operational nature that cannot be imagined on the level of the armed forces if the battle takes place in a place different than its present place. Can we, for example, imagine better facilities for the armed forces waging a battle so described were they in another place? This is in addition to the closeness of the source with the field in terms of abundance and speed in the transportation lines, supply, replenishment, training, battle operations, and other things under one military command, the experienced command in Iraq, and under a political leadership that gained experience in circumstances of struggle and jihad and in running the military, popular, and political operations for many years.

Therefore, O brother mujahidin and valiant men in the armed forces, you are waging a battle with these positive characteristics because of its description and circumstances, as well as its known complications. And victory in this battle is certain, God willing.

What days are these, during which the believers will be satisfied with the sincere endeavor and the honor of the faithful associated with any of these days. And how will it look when this belonging is a belonging to jihad and an endeavor to carry arms in the face of injustice, oppressors, infidelity, infidels, their aggressive and expansionist objectives, and their loathsome tyranny. The prime objective of this endeavor is the liberation of the dear land of Palestine and the Golan under the banner of the slogan God is great. Pride is the lot of the faithful believers, the sons of the nation; and shame and a curse on the deviants, traitors, infidels, and hypocrites.

Glory and mercy to all the martyrs of the nation and the martyrs of the armed forces. O God, protect the people, the nation, and the good believers in the world; O God protect the comrades in arms and in faith, the brave men in the armed forces, from the evil of the evil ones and the hostility of aggressors. O generous God, protect and take all the faithful mujahidin and strugglers wherever they are.

God is great. And shame to the ignominious.

May God's peace, mercy, and blessings be upon you.

Source: FBIS-NES-90-004, 7 January 1991.

16. Saddam Husayn's Message to President Bush
16 January 1991

Letter from President Saddam Husayn to "Bush," described as "written on the morning of 16 January 1991 and revised by the Revolution Command Council during an evening meeting on 16 January 1991" — read by announcer. *Baghdad Domestic Service in Arabic 0726 GMT, 17 January 1991.*

In the name of God, the merciful, the compassionate. From Saddam Husayn to Bush, enemy of God and colleague of the devil. The glorious Iraqi people and I have listened thoroughly to your hysterical statements threatening terrible consequences for Iraq and threatening aggression and destruction if Iraq fails to comply with your terms of capitulation. Accursed be you and hopeless are your objectives. You liked this method of address, and you admired this arrogant style in addressing our people and nation after you put God behind you and took the devil as your colleague. Perhaps the devil and the money spent by Fahd and the other treacherous Gulf rulers have become your masters.

It seems that because you give priority to propaganda and psychological warfare before the battle begins, you have unleashed yourself and began to make more threats to the great Iraqi people, thinking that by this method you will be able to intimidate the faithful, steadfast, and mujahid (militant) people and their valiant armed forces. No one has advised you, or you have not heeded the advice of anyone of those who know the history and heritage of the Iraqi people and the nation, because if you had known enough of the history of the people and nation and the depth of the heritage that constitutes the foundation for their lofty structure, you would not have exaggerated in counting the number of units in your navy and air force.

You would have also realized that the psychological structure of the sons of our nation, including the great Iraqi people, and their belief in fate is based in the first place on the words of God almighty in which they believe. God almighty does not love the faithful to fight under the feeling of superiority in numbers alone in their ranks against the ranks of infidels, insolent people, and aggressors.

Thus God almighty reproached and admonished the faithful who were marching under Muhammad Bin 'Abdallah to battle in the early times of Islam. God said: And of the day of Hunain; behold, your great numbers elated you, but they availed you naught (Koranic verse).

God wishes that the faithful rely first and foremost on their faith and trust in God. That is why He did not come to their aid in the Hunain battle when their great numbers elated them. God, however, helped the faithful gain victory in Badr when they were greatly outnumbered by the armies of the polytheists and atheists. God wanted to give the faithful a lesson that they and their offspring may remember.

However, you, Bush, and those who support you have forgotten that God almighty [has] instructed us to be ready for any duel with atheism, injustice, and tyranny, and to rely on Him. God said: Against them make ready your strength to the utmost of your power, including the steeds of war, to strike terror into the hearts of the enemies of God and your enemies (Koranic verse).

We have followed the dictates of God to the letter and prepared ourselves very well for battle if you choose and if Satan prods you to give battle.

When we call for peace, we abide by what God says, not out of fear. You are ignorant of history. We are being faithful to the values which God almighty has inspired in us, for we have no fear of the forces of Satan, the devil that rides on your shoulders. It seems that you are ignorant of the history of the great Iraqi people. The Iraqis fought off the armies of the British colonizers in 1920 with axes and machetes, if you know what that means. The Iraqis defeated the English and started a tradition of (words indistinct).

In the Iraqis' insistence on the values in which they believe, the other candidates, who imagined that the English had nominated them so that the English might hold the reins of government, refused. The Iraqis brought Faysal and enthroned him at first as their king. Faysal was an Arab from the land of Hejaz. He was not an Iraqi. The Iraqis did all this within the context of their insistence on their national wishes and the principles of the nation in which they believe as well as part of their insistence on God's will against the will of treason, aggression, colonialism, and atheism. If this is what the Iraqis did in 1920 and afterward, how can you imagine that threats can intimidate and frighten them when such threats come from the atheist position which you represent?

How can you imagine that threats will scare Iraqis when their planes and tanks are like yours? rather better than your tanks and the tanks of your collaborators, and that their planes are like your planes. What is more important, (words indistinct) is that they are believers and you are an atheist, unbeliever, sinful aggressor.

The Iraqis and those leading them today, Mr. Bush, remember that al-Husayn (Bin 'Ali, the third Shi'i imam) is their grandfather and their leader. They are the loyal descendants of that immortal page in the nation's history. They also believe that al-Husayn, God's peace and blessings be upon him, within the framework of what he believed — that faith is on his side and that God is with him in the fight against the adversaries — had fought thousands of people with only 70 men who had chosen his path, may their souls all rest in peace. So, why should they fear now when their force that believes in God has reached the level it has reached?

We ask God's forgiveness once again if we make a mistake in the comparison, because the basic element in power is our faith and the basic element in your weakness is your disbelief.

The Iraqis, together with all sons of our nation, also remember that Baghdad — which has become small now in your eyes, may God guide you to see what you should see correctly — the Iraqis' beautiful and faithful capital and the nation's symbol in battle, was one day, not far away for us within the framework of taking lessons, the minaret of people in faith and civilization. One man who deviated from the right path tried to make challenges. His name was Nicaphor the Byzantine. Harun al-Rashid, then the master of Baghdad and leader of the faithful gathering, returned Nicaphor letter with the following words written on it: In the name of God, the merciful, the compassionate, from Harun al-Rashid, the leader of the faithful, to Nicaphor, the Byzantine dog: Son of the infidel woman, I have read your letter. You will see and not hear the answer. Greetings.

The Iraqis, Arabs, and all Muslims are aware of all this. Moreover, they always have God on their mind and they pray to His glory. They reject injustice and refuse to bow to the unjust tyrants. This is the (?merit) of our struggling people and our great nation. You who have forgotten God imagine that threats will make our people kneel before you, but our people kneel only to God almighty.

We say that not to boast of our history, though that is an integral part of us, but to affirm that we intend, God willing, to make our present match the virtue of our past. We refuse to attribute to the American people anything that is not positive, for those people...rose to meet their humanistic duties and went out in their hundreds of thousands to denounce your aggressive policies.

Having said that, I wonder: Do you have no qualms of conscience coming from the man that is still inside you, despite your fraternity with Satan? Do you not experience nagging qualms of conscience that may deter you from evil, so as to spare you the horrible price of continuing the game that you have started? You are seemingly enjoying the threats and intimidation, as you have shown no desire to opt for dialogue and prudence that may lead to peace.

Fear God, withdraw your armies and those of your allies from the land that is sacred to Arabs and Muslims. Only this recourse, and not any other, would meet the minimum qualifications of the path that may now bring the people of the United States of America and yourself to defeat, to the woes of aggressive wars, and to hostility with Arabs and all Muslims.

Such is the recourse that has been open to you so far and is still open to you before the moment of aggression for which you are planning comes. It is to be recalled that your policy on your own land has come under no attack from the Iraqis or the sons of our people and that the dignity and future of your people, so long as they are on the right path, are safe and have never been assailed or threatened.

This is what is available to you, because we have neither threatened your land nor committed aggression against your country and people. It is you who came as aggressors, crossing the oceans and the seas to occupy the land of our sanctities, our nation's seas, and gulfs in our territories. You say that Iraq is confronting the world and not only America. In the name of faith and in the name of the believers, with the Iraqis in the forefront, we say that you and your administration (words indistinct) in your aggressive measures and in preparing the circumstances and reasons to commit the crime of aggression and war.

In truth, it suffices to cast a look at the people in the Islamic and Christian worlds and at those who represent their religious and mass positions, who stand in the line resisting your whims and upholding the human concepts, (words indistinct) your dignity has reached in the world of the devil, clamor, aggression, and atheism. Such a world is not ours and none of the (?disgraceful) factors in which you believe. This is in addition to God's values which forbid us to be part of your corrupt world or to respect that world's aggressive and (word indistinct) stand.

For the wise to discover that you are living in a world you created for yourself through money, threats, and the love of destruction and harm, they need only examine what has happened. You have spent much money on your accomplices in the crime — those who live with you in the world you created for yourself, a world that you will later burn as Nero did.

This world of yours, which you are (?persistently) talking about, would not have been created had you not spent a lot of the money of the United States, of the people of Saudi Arabia, and of others whom you forced or ordered to pay by threatening their economic interests and (word indistinct) future. If you think this is not known, you are mistaken.

Let us count the number of states that sent their forces to the land of the Muslim sanctities. And let the people of the United States, and the people of the world, answer our questions: Which state of those has not been paid by you, Fahd, or the Croesus of Kuwait? Which of them has not received the illegal money it asked for? And which of the countries that voted in favor of your resolutions at your Security Council, which advocate aggression on Iraq, has not benefited from the crime or received what would fill its belly with fire?

You and your lackeys are annoyed by the world of the righteous people, who believe in God, his divine books, his messengers, and doomsday. This world builds its solidarity through persuasion and belief in the one God and in the rights of the oppressed on earth, who have been patient with your injustice and that of your hateful world. With a clarity that might be useful to those who think before committing the crime, I want to say to you that you might be planning air strikes to achieve lightning war, thinking that Iraq will yield. You are deluding yourself. Your calculations may have led you to believe that this alone will fulfill the slogan of the lightning war you are talking about. If this is what you are thinking of, hoping that Iraq will yield to you after the air strikes and the emergence of the brokers and merchants of politics who will call for a cease-fire and bargains, and if you believe that the ground forces can be neutralized, then you are deluding yourself, and this delusion will place you in great trouble.

We say to you in the name of God, in the name of the people of

Iraq, and in the name of the nation that this illusion will be dispelled by the gathering of believers. And then you will be able to define neither the battlefield nor the type of weapons that will be used.

After the first step you take on this mad path, if you begin aggression, you will not be able to define the battlefield, arms, and time. If you can begin aggression and war, then you will not be able to define the arena of the duel, the type of the weapons that will be used, and the duration of the battle. You will find that the air force, on which you base your explanation of the lightning war, will not be alone in the battle. The battle will be prolonged and heavy blood will be shed.

Israel, the daughter of the evil ones in America, will be under the hammer. The role of political brokers, whom you believe will save your plan for a lightning war, will decline.

We say to Fahd through you — as you, regrettably, have become his master and the sovereign power in his kingdom and over his people — that until this moment we have not used the army against you. But, after using the armies of the infidels against you, everything will then become possible through our people toward you.

Our immediate support will be the heroic people in the Kingdom of Al Sa'ud, the people of Hejaz and Najd, the people of Mecca, Medina, Ta'if, Najran, Dhahran, and all the cities, villages, and the fraternal people of the eastern area. You have placed them and their wealth under the spears of the foreigner after greatly oppressing them. Regret will then not be useful to those who express regret.

The American forces will leave. Circumstances and positions will change. But those who want to live in honorable neighborliness must realize that the people of Iraq and the people of Najd and Hejaz will remain neighbors and that the believing power in Iraq will not be destroyed by the tyrants of infidelity and will get stronger, God willing.

What remains for us is to say in this letter to the American people [is] that Bush, according to his consideration and feeling, has pushed matters to a personal showdown. He has thus ignored all the chances we have given to him, and foremost of these is the 12 August initiative. Had he utilized this initiative, he would have emerged from the crisis with self-respect. After pushing matters to this point, however, we do not think that he can act objectively. The Geneva meeting proved this.

When all those Bush sent to Iraq will tell what will benefit him in the aggressive tactics that have imprisoned him in order to push things toward an impasse to justify his aggression and aggressiveness (sentence as heard).

Based on this, and so that Bush will not burn the world as Nero burned Rome, we believe that he must let the Arabs solve their affairs as they have solved other issues; that Bush must withdraw his forces and those of his allies from the holy lands of the Arabs and Muslims; and that he must look at the 12 August 1990 initiative in a new and responsible way, not as the officials in the United States did when they made statements against it even before they read its official text two hours after it was issued.

God is great. Let the lowly be accursed.

(Signed) The faithful slave of God, Saddam Husayn

(Dated) 16 January 1991, corresponding to 29 Jumada al-Akhira 1411 Hegira

Source: FBIS-NES-90-012, 17 January 1990.

17. Text of Saddam Husayn's Reply to Soviet Leader
20 January 1991

Text of letter from Saddam Husayn to Soviet President Mikhail Gorbachev in reply to Gorbachev's 18 January 1991 letter. *Baghdad INA in Arabic 1430 GMT, 21 January 1991.*

In the name of God, the merciful, the compassionate. Mr. President Gorbachev, peace be upon you.

Having read your letter and reviewed the situation and the background of relations between our two countries and two peoples, I had a feeling that I should be angry with you, or at least blame you for the method with which you tackled the issues that you described as serious and dramatic, and the means you proposed for protecting Iraq from destruction.

After remembering that the international community today is living under, or rather falling in one way or another under the mercy of the US law of hegemony and domination, with a few exceptions here and there, my anger abated and I desisted from leveling any blame here in my letter.

We, Mr. President, would like to state a fact that cannot be overemphasized, namely, that we are as free as when our mothers gave birth to us and as God created us from the earth. Because we are free men and we insist on retaining our freedom, we reject the US law of hegemony and domination. We are not the ones who have committed aggression against the United States and waged war against it. So we should not be asked to make statements that would make the United States appear to be twisting our steadfast will and that would tempt it to continue its blackmail and arrogance in our region and the world, based on the notion that everyone must submit to its law of hegemony over the world

From the very beginning, we have been drawing the attention of people who care for freedom and sovereignty and those who care about implementing the law of the only living God in relations among peoples. We have always emphasized the importance of dialogue among nations because it is important among people. Then and only then, and when the method of equitable dialogue is used, the human mind would be able to find a solution to all the region's problems, which are linked together like cause and effect. This is especially so if the dialogue is given a healthy atmosphere and mankind is provided with reassurance.

You might remember, Mr. President, that as we recall the requirements of our responsibility, which we do not forget — as Bush and the failures who encouraged him to commit his aggression and to hold man and mankind in contempt have forgotten - we say that because of our human responsibility toward security and stability in the world, we submitted our initiative on 12 August 1990, which your government said was positive in the beginning. You did not pursue your efforts to put it within the framework of serious discussion. You remember how Bush rejected it only two hours after we broadcast it on the air without even bothering to ask for an official copy of the initiative. He might not have even read it as disseminated by world news agencies.

You also remember, Mr. President, how the United States and its media urged the destruction of our military and scientific power even before 2 August, and how it had been denying our people bread as of March 1990 by a decision of the US Congress and Administration. You remember how Bush instigated his treasonous rulers, such as Jabir al-Ahmad, the former shaykh of Kuwait, to plot against Iraq.

This is part of what we wanted to remind you of in this letter. It is only part of what should be recalled about the treacherous plot and the unjust aggression. We say this so you can remember that the US president is conspiratorial and treacherous, that he has a grudge against the Arabs, and that he is working to stifle any noble voice that may demand the liberation of Palestine and an end to the suffering of the Arab people of Palestine.

Bush has committed aggression and must pay the price of his

aggression if he continues to indulge in it. The punishment of God, the one and only God the almighty, the powerful, and the great, will be his punishment.

Therefore, your letter should have been addressed to the tyrant Bush and not to Saddam Husayn and his aggrieved people.

God is Great, God is great, God is great. Accursed be Bush and his henchmen.

(Dated) 20 January 1991

Source: FBIS-NES-91-014, 22 January 1991.

18. "Mother of Battles" Airs Saddam Husayn CNN Interview 28 January 1991

Interview with President Saddam Husayn by CNN correspondent Peter Arnett in Baghdad on 28 January 1991 — recorded. Saddam speaks in Arabic with alternating passage-by-passage superimposed translation into English; Arnett speaks in English with alternating passage-by-passage superimposed translation into Arabic — processed from the Arabic. *Baghdad Mother of Battles Radio Network in Arabic 1759 GMT, 2 February 1991.*

(Arnett:) Mr. President Saddam Husayn, I came to this meeting in a car (word indistinct) through the dark roads of Baghdad. (words indistinct) by the US attacks on the Iraqi power stations. The US air raids on your country are many and the US (?command...words indistinct) that they are winning the first round of this war. What do you say to this?

(Saddam:) We say that light emerges from darkness. Whenever the US Administration expects that it is covering Baghdad with darkness, it will face the light inside the hearts of the Iraqi people, based on a deep belief in the one God. (Words indistinct) brought by the US Administration (words indistinct). You see that the picture now is different from what they were talking about before they started the aggression against us. What happened will (word indistinct) the U.S. Administration and the specialists who are helping it are saying that they are winning the first round. We will leave this as a matter for the American people to decide, because the American people (words indistinct).

So we leave the assessment to the people of the United States, all free nations in the world, and to you too, on whether they have actually won in the first round, or whether disgrace befell them the moment they decided to make this decision. We believe that they have been defeated by simply signing their decision, because they signed an unjust decision. The days and weeks have come — we are now in the second week — and the day-to-day details of the developments will emerge to show the defeat (words indistinct). Winning and losing does not hinge on winning or losing a battle quickly, because winning depends on gaining the satisfaction of the one and only God (passage indistinct). This is the [criterion] we follow.

(Arnett:) You have had an eight-year-long war with Iran. (Words indistinct), throughout that war, throughout that time, (?Iraq) was not affected or harmed in the same way it has been harmed this time. Therefore, how do you evaluate this period of conflict (words indistinct)?

(Saddam:) We must not forget that our people have never been as pure in their spirits as they are now. Our armed forces have never been as determined throughout (?their history...words indistinct) and throughout all the difficult circumstances, which they faced and which they had to deal with.

(Arnett:) A large number of Iraqi planes are now (?landing) in Iranian airports. The (?announced) figure is (figure indistinct) aircraft. Can you shed some light on the reasons behind this (word indistinct)?

(Saddam:) Regardless of the figures which you hear, and which we know, what is important is that Iraq and Iran are two Muslim neighboring countries. And, regardless of the past circumstances, these ties will remain (words indistinct) relations between the two countries. Since the battle is now between faith and infidelity, between right and wrong, between treachery and honesty, between justice and fairness, and oppression and hegemony and aggression, then do not expect that there will be Muslim countries which are not with us in such a battle. Naturally, when some of Iraq's planes find they have to land in this or that Islamic country, they would do so in that spirit and in such a (word indistinct).

(Arnett:) But will these planes continue to be used in this war? Will they return to Iraq to be used in this conflict?

(Saddam:) In all cases, we respect the laws and will of (word indistinct).

(Arnett:) (Words indistinct) can these planes (words indistinct)?

(Saddam:) If the (?circumstance ... words indistinct).

(Arnett:) The other issue now is (words indistinct) oil in the Gulf, the oil slick in the Gulf. (Words indistinct) claims that the bombing of the Iraqi tankers caused this slick. But the United States says the Iraqi officials opened the oil pipes and let it flow into the Gulf (words indistinct).

(Saddam:) The fact is that the United States hit a number of tankers which were loaded with oil. This is a fact. The Western media did not deny this fact. (Words indistinct) it must have then been aware that these tankers were loaded with oil. Add to this that the United States attacked some oil installations. Therefore, these are the facts (words indistinct). Therefore, the United States is not concerned with preventing the leaking of oil in this or that place, whether on land or in the sea. Nor is it concerned with the negative effects on the environment in the sea or other places. When it does so (words indistinct). Hence the US Administration cannot allege that it is doing this within the framework of necessity and legitimate self-defense (words indistinct). Therefore, if the military field commanders view the use of oil (?as part) of the legitimate right to self-defense and defending the homeland (words indistinct) or in any other form, then such commanders will have the right to do so. Thus, this is the picture now (words indistinct).

(Arnett:) Are you saying that (words indistinct) open and the oil (word indistinct) the Gulf was really a military maneuver?

(Saddam:) I did not say this. I have said that the United States used oil without being forced to do so. The indisputable fact is that the United States has hit oil tankers full of oil. It knew that they were full of oil, and it knew that when this oil spills into the water, it causes damage. When these tankers were hit, they were inside Iraq's territorial waters. The United States also hit oil pipelines and announced this publicly. It hit the loading platforms. These platforms are in Iraq's territorial waters. US experts know that when they hit loading platforms and destroy the oil pipelines in these platforms, oil will leak and flow into Iraqi territorial waters. This act cannot be regarded as an act of necessity. However, if the Iraqis use oil for defensive purposes, even in the sea, they are justified in doing so. It is certain that the future will show that the United States is responsible for this.

(Arnett:) Then what you are saying, Mr. President, is that you reserve the right to use oil as a military weapon in the open sea?

(Saddam:) I said what I have said. Everything is clear.

(Arnett:) Another issue (?in the minds of Americans) — American prisoners of war and (?those) of the multinational force. It is reported that your government will use prisoners of war — pilots — as human shields in strategic installations. This was announced last week. Is this what actually happened, and will it continue?

(Saddam:) What we announced was an official declaration. But are there people in the West who can still talk about ethics and law? Take this example (words indistinct). Do you remember what (words indistinct) before Iraq made a declaration banning foreigners from travel to prevent the outbreak of war? Do you remember what was said about our decision? It was described as an immoral, illegal, and inhuman decision. The West was bragging about its humanity, and some Western rulers were (words indistinct) such allegations to people who had not yet discovered their true nature fully. Do you remember this? Do you know what they are doing now, those same (words indistinct) who were criticizing our decisions? Do you know that they are detaining the Iraqis, even the students who went to study in the West? They are being detained, and the decision to detain them has been made public. Do you know the restrictions imposed on the Americans of Arab origin — on the Iraqis and the Maghreb people who hold various citizenships throughout the West, in a number of Western countries? A number of Arabs who previously held Arab nationalities became citizens of Western nations. However, in the wake of the war, severe restrictions were imposed on them in violation of the rules of these countries, including your own country, the United States. Is this not a demonstration of a double standard? Do you notice how long it took for these double standards to surface? They took 10 days to emerge. Do you see how much of the West's defects we have exposed in such a short time?

Rest assured that we feel that you in the West need our steadfastness and rejection of this arrogance, which comes out from (words indistinct). We feel that the human being inside you, that your humanity as Americans, as citizens, and that your humanity as Frenchmen and Britons in the West needs our position in rejecting hegemony and double standards more than it needs the decision of hegemony and double standards emerging from (words indistinct)... need to expose double standards. The world needs someone to tell the one who carries the biggest stick in the world that the stick that you carry in your hand cannot bring down the house of God and cannot (word indistinct) the humanity of man. This is what you need in the West. You do not need to see your planes kill a large number of children, women, and elderly people in Iraq. (Word indistinct) are people, and people do not need this. But Bush, or the devil inside Bush, needs this.

(Arnett:) [Words indistinct] You said that (words indistinct) international norms and the Geneva Convention does not fall in line with the use of these prisoners of war as human shields.

(Saddam:) (Words indistinct) the Iraqi students (words indistinct). Therefore, these double standards prevail in the countries which call themselves the number one countries in the world. These countries are asking the small countries, which they describe as Third World nations, to apply the law. But they consider themselves above the law, and exempted from it.

(Arnett:) We believe that you visited the battlefront occasionally. We have seen pictures of you down in Kuwait. Could you tell us what it is like to be at the front and what the battlefront situation (words indistinct)?

(Saddam:) The men of faith there are holding steadfast. (Words indistinct) they went there to drive the Iraqi army from Kuwait. (Passage indistinct) I do not want to insult anyone but I merely say that this is what is found in the dictionary, that any person who does not tell the truth is a liar. The Iraqi army is in Kuwait. It is certain that you Americans used to think that the attack would be launched against the army — the attacks of the 16th (16 January) against the 19th (governorate — reference to Kuwait; words indistinct). He did not begin the attack against the armed forces in the 19th (governorate — (Kuwait),but in Baghdad. He did not launch it against the military forces, but against security and economic installations. Doubtless you remember, as a journalist, how many assurances were issued by the White House media about the destruction of Iraqi nuclear power. Did you not ask yourself why? Did you not as an American realize that the battle, therefore, was not for the sake of Kuwait, but for other reasons? These are the same reasons for which the US Administration incited the Kuwaiti rulers to conspire against us before 2 August. They are also the same reasons for which the US Administration decided to prevent the sending of grain and food to Iraq five months before the events of 2 August. For the same reasons, the US Administration raised the slogan of boycotting Iraq technologically and in matters of security. This happened more than five months before the events of 2 August. Unfortunately, the ordinary US citizen could not put together all those measures which the US Administration adopted before the events of 2 August to reach the same conclusion we reached before that date. For that reason, Bush was able to lie to the American people. However, we will help you to unmask the liars. We will do this with these facts. The facts are revealed now. President Bush cannot deny that he began the attacks on scientific and economic installations, and not on the army in Kuwait (passage indistinct).

(Arnett:) The military experts of the US military command and (words indistinct) are saying that they can probably destroy your (words indistinct) in Kuwait with bombardment — with aerial bombing — and may not need to invade or reinvade, but just mop up the remainder of your forces. (Words indistinct) how can they survive the massive bombing that (words indistinct) can bring to bear?

(Saddam:) This is what we said and what we warned of before the war began. Do you remember? I think you remember (words indistinct). He made a statement that it would be a matter of 24 hours. Then (?Husni... words indistinct) a person must not give advice in which he does not believe. It appears that Husni has taken it upon himself to say that the Arab man cannot endure in battle more than 24 hours. You may recall that some people used to say it would be a matter of 72 hours. Regardless of anything, (words indistinct) the days and months. This was not the aim (words indistinct). We were seeking to spare humanity (?further bloodshed). For this reason, we were frank in explaining the facts. We said that our people had (words indistinct). They believed that dialogue was the way which leads to solutions that would enable humanity to avoid warfare. We said that a person must not delude himself into believing that when war starts it will be a war of hours, days, or weeks.

At any rate, we said that when war begins, a lot of blood will be shed. We also said we did not want this. We have no interest in seeing any world leader getting involved in a war and then miserably failing. Do you remember what the Western leaders, including President Bush, used to say? They used to say that they were going to enter the war without one American suffering injuries. Has this happened? (Words indistinct) the war is at its (?beginning). Only 10 days. Is it true that no American has been injured? What will happen if the war (words indistinct)? Therefore, those who have miscalculated in this war must alone confront the people's (?questions) and public opinion.

As for the men in Kuwait (words indistinct). It is not a matter of who has more weapons. The issue is who will be defeated and who will not be defeated, and who has Satan on his side and who has God on his side. Who crossed thousands of kilometers to come to whose homeland? Who came to occupy the land and sanctities of the other? The answer is clear. Do you believe that the pilots who came to bombard Baghdad, dropping bombs from great heights without knowing where they will fall, were (?happy)? I saw some of them on the television screen. Of course, those who were killed were more numerous than those who appeared on television. Perhaps you know that it is a natural thing that the ratio of staying alive in such cases is approximately (words indistinct). When the time comes for you to receive the corpses of your sons you will know (words indistinct). I asked those who saw them: Did you not ask them if they felt regret for what they had done? They said yes, and when I asked what the answer was they said some of them had wept. Some of them were in bad shape. I do not want to speak of this. (?If you now look at) the men manning the anti-aircraft guns and fighting against Bush, you will find that each of them is proud of what he has done in defense of Iraq and the values it represents.

Some of them were in positions on which bombs fell like rain, but not a single Iraqi left his anti-aircraft gun with which he was confronting the US planes. This was particularly true the first day, the second, the third, and the fourth day. From these examples you may predict the outcome of the duel on the ground, if the aggressive armies attack our valiant men in the 19th governorate. What remains is one question dealing with how matters were before 2 August and after 2 August, until the night of 15 January (word indistinct). After war broke out on that night of 15 January (as heard), (word indistinct) how can a people of 18 million confront all this massive hostile power with honor? (Words indistinct.) How will this be? Had this people not been sure of the justice of their cause, they would not have resisted in such circumstances (words indistinct) those who seek the truth should pay attention to such a manifestation. When their attention is drawn to this manifestation, then they will be guided toward the solution through dialogue and not through war.

Then, one would be able to discover many, many more facts.

(Arnett:) You mentioned dialogue. At what level are you talking about? Is dialogue possible now on this issue? (Words indistinct) delay the comprehensive battles should be (word indistinct) sooner or later?

(Saddam:) A dialogue, that is to talk with people and not with the US president. I am speaking to you as a citizen. I am speaking about honest dialogue with people and not with the aggressors and the treacherous. As a people, we (words indistinct). But the evil ones will shoulder the responsibility (words indistinct). I am speaking about human laws that should govern the relationships among people.

(Arnett:) What do you say to governments, to people around the world today who are seeking a peaceful solution? Is it possible? Is there more hope now?

(Saddam:) This question should be addressed to Bush by you, the American people. Bush used dialogue as a tactic. You know that we are the ones who proposed dialogue, and he rejected dialogue. He appeared on television suddenly to say that he wants dialogue. We immediately discovered that he had decided on war. His new talk about dialogue is only a cover to say to those who say to him that he has not exhausted the path of dialogue that he has held dialogue and they did not respond. This is exactly what took place, as we have said. All that we have said from 2 August until now has been achieved. Do you remember what we said, that keeping foreigners and not allowing them to travel would prevent the war?

Do you remember what the charlatan Western politicians said? They said that keeping the Westerners and preventing them from traveling would make war happen and that Westerners' travel would not make the war happen. The issue has become clear now. It is now in the past. We do not regret a decision we made because we make decisions only when we are convinced. However, had we kept the 5,000 Westerners and Japanese in Iraq, would Bush have struck Baghdad?

When we made the decision and allowed the Westerners to travel, we were not scared. We were not intimidated by threats from anyone, (words indistinct) because we fear no one. We made the decision out of respect for the opinion of the average citizen rather than that of politicians. So that cards could not be mixed and colors could not be blurred, we decided to allow all to travel so that our battle would not involve a blurred vision or confused cards. However, I referred to this for a reason — to prove to you that certain Western politicians are playing the game of double standards with us (word indistinct) and not the game, the action, or the behavior of statesmen.

(Arnett:) (Words indistinct) you mentioned several times if the land battle comes, and yet it seems clear from what Western governments in the multinational forces are saying that it is a matter of when the battle comes.

(Saddam:) Anyway, the war is going on. So why speak about a ground battle or any other type? The war is going on. Now what has been achieved? Has Bush gained victory? I say that Bush was defeated from the very first moment he signed the decision to wage war. He has created a situation (words indistinct). I, too, (word indistinct) that you are ashamed now, and if I were in your place, I would certainly be ashamed. I am confident that every American now feels ashamed inside himself. And as the war goes on, the shame will turn into pain, and the pain will turn into revolution against those who deceived him. The American is a human being and he asks himself the following questions: Are these the values of the superpower, the United States? Are these the values about which Bush is speaking? (Words indistinct) that of mobilizing 29 countries and have his armies cross the Atlantic Ocean, the oceans, and the seas to attack a nation of 18 million people? Do you feel now that you still are a superpower? Do you feel that you are a superpower while you hold out your hand to collect funds for your armies that you have dispatched to attack us, and while the president of the most important superpower boasts that he has come to attack a nation of 18 million? These are the factors that make the (US) Administration internally defeated. The moment it signed the war decision, it was defeated. This made America retreat from the position of a superpower.

(Arnett:) (Words indistinct) war in Kuwait. How long do you think it will last? And how many casualties (words indistinct) the multinational forces?

(Saddam:) God knows how long it will take. But what we are certain of is that the Iraqis will fight in a way that will be admired by the human side of the American personality.

A lot of blood (words indistinct) will be shed. A lot of blood has been shed already. Certainly, the officials who decided to carry out the aggression do not ask how many Iraqis are martyred in that aggression. I was following their statements before the hostile military action. None of the senior officials has expressed his genuine desire to avoid the shedding of Iraqi blood. They deceived their parliaments by saying there would be no American casualties, or that if there were casualties, they would be few. They also said there would be no British or French casualties and that if there were casualties, there would be very few of them. However, when we say that a lot of blood will be shed, we mean French, English, American, and of course Saudi citizens' and people's blood — all those taking part in the fighting — and (word indistinct) Iraqi blood.

Do not be deceived once again by the accursed politicians who present the battle to you piecemeal, speaking first of an air battle, then telling you to be hopeful and wait until the ground battle takes place. War is war. War has started, and you must count the days, weeks, and months for them and always ask them: Did you not say that the war would last only a few days? Therefore, you have miscalculated, just as you miscalculated before.

(Arnett:) You have unconventional weapons like (words indistinct) chemical weapons. Will you use chemical weapons in a land war in Kuwait?

(Saddam:) We will use weapons that match those used against us by our enemy. I believe that by now you are (word indistinct) that we have done all we had previously said.

(Arnett:) The multinational (word indistinct) said they would not use chemical weapons against you. Would that mean that if they do not use them, you do not use them?

(Saddam:) I said that we will use weapons that are equivalent to those used against us. In any case, we will not (word indistinct) Iraq. We will not accept Kuwait to be (?penetrated). Iraq's borders extend from Zakho to the sea.

(Arnett:) You have been launching missile attacks against Israel. And as you (word indistinct) to the media (words indistinct) everybody involved in this war.

(Saddam:) All the forces raiding Baghdad now are Israeli. (Words indistinct) against Baghdad because Zionism, which played in the corridors of the White House, pushed (words indistinct). If it were not for Zionism and its hostility to Arabs, why would America decide to withhold food from the Iraqis five months before the 2 August events? This is the battle of Zionism, but Zionism is fighting us with your blood (words indistinct). If it is not using some of its weapons now, it is because it wants to (words indistinct) so that it can have the upper hand when the war comes to an end. Zionism (words indistinct). If it were not for Zionism, you would certainly have not come to occupy the Ka'ba and the Prophet Muhammad's shrine (words indistinct) and commit aggression against the (word indistinct). We will not be deceived by (word indistinct). Therefore, you can certainly admit that we said that if Baghdad were hit, we would strike Tel Aviv. We (words indistinct) Tel Aviv that we know the entire game. We tell them: Leave the land of Jerusalem and stop slaughtering Palestinians. Israel is occupying our land (?in the name of) Arabs. It is occupying the lands of Palestine, the Golan Heights, part of Lebanon. Therefore, Israel is an occupier and an aggressor against Arabs. Therefore, this is our message: The missiles and the causes for (words indistinct).

(Arnett:) (Words indistinct) chemical warheads (word indistinct) Scud missiles and that (word indistinct) capable (words indistinct) chemical weapons (words indistinct) and even on, say, civilian targets in Saudi Arabia.

(Saddam:) (Words indistinct) why do you avoid calling things by their proper names? Scud is your own system, which has a range of 270 km. As for this, it is an Iraqi missile called al-Husayn. Its twin brother, al-'Abbas, has a range of approximately 1,000 km. and we are developing it to be ready for use in the numbers we might need. Some specialists are aware of this (word indistinct).

I do not (words indistinct). I do not mean the American citizen. However, we can say that (words indistinct). The major claim is that (words indistinct). Certainly they will remember the Iraqis now, and they are 18 million (words indistinct) able to fight indefinitely until victory is recorded for good against evil. Do you know (?al-Husayn)?

(Arnett:) I know the name of the missile.

(Saddam:) I knew (words indistinct...(laughs).

(Arnett:) But I do not know if it has a chemical warhead and if you are prepared to use that against Israel (words indistinct) Saudi Arabia.

(Saddam:) It can carry nuclear, chemical, and biological warheads.

(Arnett:) (Words indistinct) conventional explosions in your missiles so far.

(Saddam:) I have said that we use weapons that match those used by the opposite side. We are people who remember the values of our forefathers. (Word indistinct) in difficult circumstances, everyone remembers the values of his ancestors. Despite all that air superiority, we were not shaken. We have not deviated from the concept of balanced conduct. (Words indistinct) use conventional warheads in your missiles? Is that coming? We hope there will be no (words indistinct). We hope we will not be forced to do the imperative.

(Arnett:) (Words indistinct) when you (word indistinct) mentioned that your missile (word indistinct) system (words indistinct). Can you give us any information about the destruction that your nuclear facility has undergone in the bombing?

(Saddam): Do you believe that this is possible? These things (words indistinct) the Americans are now imposing restrictions on you and on news of the soldiers in Saudi Arabia. And they impose (word indistinct) details (words indistinct) on the course of military operations (words indistinct). And this happens in the country of democracy, as they call it in America. Do you want a dictatorship, as you call Iraq, to divulge such serious secrets? What counts is that the Iraqi man is full of faith. He has faith and is full of self-confidence. He is convinced every hour — with every hour of the fighting he is more convinced, through additional factors, that right is on his side. What they destroy (words indistinct) a strong, faithful, and living people who can give what is more (word indistinct). No one will donate anything to us to make up for all that has been and will be destroyed. We built that with sleepless nights, patience, perseverance, and sincerity in work. When we say we, we mean all the people of Iraq (words indistinct). When the Iraqis say we, they mean the citizens, not the leadership.

(Arnett:) You said that (words indistinct) the mother of all battles. Every field commander before any battle (words indistinct) has doubts about the outcome of the battle ahead. Do you have any doubts whatsoever that you will win?

(Saddam:) Not even 1 percent. I just want to clarify one thing (words indistinct) when we call it the mother of battles. We are not writing the military history, because the battle has not yet taken place (words indistinct). Right will win over wrong. We believe that God is on our side. Is there a greater battle than the battle in which the commander is God on one side and Satan on the other side?

See for yourself, America, the superpower, Great Britain — I use the names that you use to describe these countries — and France, a major power. All the powers that possess big weapons along with the countries of dirty money are grouped together against Iraq. With this in mind, can any person not be convinced that God is on our side? (Words indistinct) God who made the elephant reach Ka'ba and then ordered it to turn back (words indistinct) is capable of defeating all the armies of the aggressors.

(Arnett:) You have invited me (words indistinct) CNN here to conduct this interview with you. What do you hope (words indistinct) this interview will have on the United States and the world?

(Saddam:) (Words indistinct) I have said what I believe to be the truth. You tell the Americans that we wish them well and we hope that none of their sons will die. All Iraqis are grateful to all good Americans who demonstrated in the United States against the war and to all good and honorable citizens in France, Germany, Spain, Italy, and everywhere else. We are attentively following this noble level of humanity that opposes the hostile policy that is being made in the corridors influenced by criminal Zionism. All Iraqis, including the children in Iraqi hospitals who have been injured by the bombs dropped on them, are following this attentively. We will continue to distinguish between the evil decision by the administrations influenced by Zionism and the stand adopted by the people of (words indistinct). Just as we make a pledge to God, our people, the sons of our nation, we also make a pledge to good people in America, Europe, Japan, the USSR, and everywhere else in the world — in the countries described as developed and those called Third World countries — that we will not forget the good people, who will discover day after day that they are right when (words indistinct) against our people and nation.

I am pleased to have met with you. Thank you for having listened with an open mind. (Words indistinct) Thank you.

Source: FBIS-NES-91-025, 6 February 1991.

19. Saddam Husayn Delivers Message to Iraqis, Arabs, and Muslims
10 February 1991

Commentator: The leader struggler President Saddam Husayn has described the steadfast struggling people of Iraq as a vanguard of the force of the faithful. In a historic speech tonight addressed to the Iraqi people, the Arab nation, and the Islamic peoples, the president saluted the resistance the valiant Iraqis have demonstrated to the planes of aggression and the missiles of shame.

His excellency praised the will of steadfastness, the faith, and the light in the hearts of the Iraqis and their generous, faithful readiness to refuse to abandon their role which God has ordained for them and to respond to God's desire humbly and faithfully.

The president struggler Saddam Husayn said that with every day and hour that passes, the Iraqis are clinging to what they believe in and their brightness is increasing before the whole world. What is more important, the president said, is that their status in the eyes of God the almighty is being strengthened and firmly established. *Baghdad INA in Arabic 1947 GMT, 10 February 1991.*

The following is the text of the struggler president's speech:

President Saddam Husayn: O faithful, struggling, patient, great Iraqi people, when I speak to the Iraqis, I speak through them to every Muslim, every Arab, and every individual who sees in this people the true model whom God, may He be praised, has chosen to play the role that He wants and with which He is satisfied. O great people, I say behold now that we have entered with unshakable faith and unparalleled constancy in righteousness into the seventh month with all the great glory that its days carry and all the glory that was promised by the days of the months that preceded it. We have entered this seventh month after the first day of the path of the battle of righteousness and faith against falsehood and atheism.

We are now in the seventh month since the day when atheism and falsehood reached a most extensive agreement to implement an unjust siege on the Iraqi people. They did not even make allowances for the exceptions they themselves laid down in this siege. They violated even the feeble barrier by which they wanted to deceive those who could be deceived by their claims. The siege affected food, medicine, and even baby milk. Seven months have passed since the confrontation began on a most extensive level between the tyrannical opposing force and the forward struggler power of faith, whose great march is represented by the patient, struggler, faithful Iraqi people. The Iraqi people have patience in good times and in hard times, and when fortitude is called for. "These are the truly faithful and the pious people." Verily speaks the almighty.

After the parties (groups that opposed the Prophet Muhammad in the early stages of Islam) and the Arabians (the groups that joined them in fighting against Muhammad), who had earlier resisted the call of God and his Prophet Muhammad, God's prayers and peace be upon him, discovered that the siege would not make them abandon their faith, they thought that arms could wrest faith from the hearts of the faithful and would put the latter in a state of shame and humiliation while they would be in a boastful position.

Curse their spite and their actions. They committed their treacherous crime in their armed aggression on the night of 16 January. Its darkness will be all that they will reap. It is not the sole witness to the deception and vileness in their treacherous hearts, which are devoid of faith and isolated from all that is pure and all that faithful hearts aspire to.

On the other hand, the torches of the valiant men who are resisting the planes of aggression and the missiles of shame will remain the most prominent sign of the will of endurance, faith, and light in the hearts and souls of the Iraqis and their great belief-based readiness not to relinquish their role, which God has willed for them and to which they have responded faithfully and obediently.

O valiant men and glorious women, your enemy has imagined that he is capable of achieving what he wants to turn back the cycle of history and the accumulated belief of the faithful linked to it through the unjust siege. When his hopes were dashed and his calculations failed, he took the road of armed aggression in a direct manner. We have now entered the fourth week of this aggression. With every hour and day that passes the Iraqis are becoming more committed to what they believe in and more radiant before the whole world. The most important thing is that their place with God almighty is getting firmer and more sublime, because jihad is the road to this glory.

Now that the strugglers have struggled, God almighty does not make a distinction between the upright and martyrs on the one hand, and the Iraqi strugglers on the other. God's great will always prevails.

Every hour and day that has passed since the beginning of the siege against the gathering of vanguard believers in Iraq is an hour and day of defeat for the gathering of atheism, oppression, and tyranny. The beginning of the first dark night of each new month is a mark of darkness for their lost hopes and a sign of frustration for their defeated gathering. The light of every new moon at the beginning of a new month is a sign of a great and certain victory for the struggling gathering of believers, and for all believers, and is absolute proof to anyone who needs proof that God is alive, capable, and great.

The Friday prayer in each week of the weeks of fighting is a celebration for the believers, who have kept their faith, which has been dipped in chaste blood, and is a great and remarkable victory for them and for mankind over tyranny, treason, and shame represented by the United States, the Arabian traitors, and the unjust and defeated allies, who are the slaves of Bush.

Therefore, those of the sons of our nation and the good-hearted people who are searching for victory in terms of hours, days, and months, must not search for it outside this great and immortal chapter of the time that has passed. Victory is present in every hour, day, and week since the first hour of the siege, and the first hour and day of the armed showdown, and until the last hour and day, when God permits the end of this war stamped with His great victory. God willing.

Those who ask when and how and where the aggression was defeated must look for the answer in the first moments of the necessity — that was how the leader of the largest country, which he calls the greatest among countries, describe[d] it — to make the decision to go to war in the wake of the boycott decision. This decision was made instead of a decision to hold a dialogue. He also assembled against us those whom he could assemble after he saw the power of America small in his eyes, or perhaps God willed it to be so. In this way he lost his credibilty and made the United States lose its credibility as the largest or greatest power, as he describes it. Bush lost his credibility after he lost the power of conviction and the power to persuade by dialogue to avoid the use of force. He lost his credibility on the day he brought the weapon of confrontation which the West had built up against the entire Warsaw Pact to confront a single Third World country — a country of Arabs to which they used to refuse to attach the importance which God wanted for them as human beings and proprietors of a divine message.

The president of the United States lost his credibility and made America lose its credibility as the greatest power in his confrontation with the fortress of faith in Iraq. He started calling on others to join him from every direction, but we called on no one except the faithful people who find that their position must definitely be on our side. We called on the assistance of no one against them except God, the merciful, the one and only, as we prayed to Him, may He be praised.

Bush and his henchmen, and those Arabs who are more atheistic and hypocritical than he, were defeated in every moment, every minute, every hour, and every day after the starting line was crossed. You were victorious, O valiant Iraqis and glorious Iraqi women, in every moment, minute, hour, day, week, and month after the first moment in this battle. All the faithful and good people in the world were victorious with you over tyranny, corruption, atheism, and infidelity.

With God's help, and through a miracle coming from God more than 1,400 years after the appearance of the bright Islamic message, you, strugglers, have proved that the one God exists, that faith and the faithful are in good shape, and that, when God permits, the oppressed can score victory over tyranny. This happened when Moses, God's peace be upon him, won over the soldiers of the pharaoh after God had sunk them in the sea; when the values of Jesus triumphed over the corruption and ill will of the Jews and the betrayal of Judas; when God enabled the Ka'ba to triumph over the elephant, which they brought to sabotage God's house but turned round and retreated upon God's orders; when messenger Muhammad triumphed over al-Ahzab (confederation of Jews and unbelievers) and emerged victorious in the battle of Badr; and when the Muslims destroyed the entities of the two superpowers that alone oppressed and enslaved the world and had established their entities on oppression and vice.

Through your miracle in the name of God, you, Iraqis, have proved that God is present, alive, and everlasting. There is no explanation other than this for your legendary steadfastness and the defeat of your enemies, knowing all the force they prepared and the force you prepared in return. It is the unmistakable promise, O brave men and glorious women of Iraq. The false Arabs thought it was too much for you to be described as glorious, so they started planning to desecrate glory by their losers' life; shame on what they are doing.

It is the promise of ultimate victory, soon, God willing. Nothing remains but that which consolidates the faith of the faithful and brings final victory closer, and that which deepens the infidelity of the infidels, takes them further away from faith, and brings them closer to the edge of the abyss. They will all fall in this abyss, and not one of them will return to the illuminated place or enjoy the mercy of God and the believers. The Iraqis and all the believers, on the other hand, will take the position granted to them by God almighty in life and in the afterlife.

All the requirements of a free and honorable life will return to them. Nothing remains between them and this life except the final touch which will reward their patience, perseverance, and struggle. It will be the fruit of their patience and of their creative effectiveness, added to the effectiveness of these great people, their armed forces, their honest and pious popular army, and their holy war forces. It is the chapter of an additional time which will liberate the souls and all precious things. It will also liberate the holy places of the Arabs and Muslims in Mecca, Medina, and Jerusalem. It will place the faithful Arab men and the Iraqis in the front ranks and prepare for them a future and a life that no one can disturb.

And those of the people of the book who aided them—God did take them from their strongholds and cast terror into their hearts, so that some ye slew, and some ye made prisoners. And He made you heirs of their lands, their houses, and their goods, and of a land which ye had not frequented before. And God has power over all things (Koranic verse). Verily, God said the truth.

Mercy for our innocent martyrs. Greetings of appreciation and love to the struggling sons of our nation wherever they are, who are fighting the group of infidels and meting out to them the punishment they deserve, or who are demonstrating to denounce the aggression and affirm their great affiliation, or who are saying the truth as it should be said in any influential arena.

Greetings of appreciation and love to every Muslim who has been pained to see the group of infidels and liars killing and maiming Iraqi children, women, and old men, and who has rejected this aggression against this nation that has brought to him the Koran, which preaches the orthodox principles of Islam.

Greetings to every man in this world who has rejected the policy of the armadas of evil and aggression pursued by the assistants of Satan, namely Bush and his allies and who has joined mankind in rejecting this aggression and calling for peace.

Special greetings to the beloved ones in Palestine, Golan, and occupied Lebanon. Special greetings to our brothers in Jordan, Sudan, Algeria, Yemen, Mauritania, Morocco, Tunisia, and Libya. Greetings to everyone who has attacked falsehood and uttered a sincere and honest word. Greetings to everyone with a clean and white hand. God is great. God is great. God is great. Accursed be the lowly.

Source: FBIS-NES-91-028, 11 February 1991.

20. Saddam Husayn Addresses Nation on His Initiative 21 February 1991

Full recording of address by President Saddam Husayn on 21 February 1991, place not given. *Baghdad Domestic Service in Arabic 1500 GMT, 21 February 1991.*

In the name of God, the compassionate, the merciful. Which, then, is the best? He that layeth his foundation on piety to God and His good pleasure? Or he that layeth his foundation on an undermined cliff of sand, ready to crumble to pieces? And it doth crumble to pieces with him, into the fire of hell. And God guideth not people that do wrong. The foundation of those who so build is never free from suspicion and shakiness in their hearts, until their hearts are cut to pieces. And God is all-knowing, wise (Koranic verses).

O great people, O stalwart men in our valiant armed forces, O faithful, honest Muslims, wherever you may be, O people wherever faith in God has found its way to your hearts, and wherever it found what embodies it in the sincerity of your intentions and deeds, O lovers of humanity, virtue, and fairness, who reject aggressiveness, injustice, and unfairness, in difficult circumstances and their events, some people — more often than not — lose the connection with the beginning and preoccupy themselves with the results, or forget, when there are resemblances, the connection between any result and the reasons that gave rise to those events, and on whose basis those results were based. Furthermore, in difficult circumstances, which difficulty is hard to describe, the mind and consciousness are generally preoccupied with what influences the life of the individual concerned with that circumstance. Thus, he bases his opinion and position on it without connecting every individual case with what is collective. The future is even absent at times or is not given very great importance as an indispensable weight for assessing the

(?influence) of each case, regardless of whether the case or individual item being assessed is connected to the past and present or to the reasons and beginnings, or whether it is part of the results. And regardless of whether it was part of the simple results and individual items, with limited effect, or of the major results that have a comprehensive effect that go beyond the individual, a number of individuals, or only a specific sector in the society, to the society as a whole and where it goes beyond the transient and quick-moving present to the future as a whole (sentence as heard).

Some have either completely forgotten these influential facts in the life of man, whether in this or that direction, or the presence of these facts in their minds has become weak. Many facts between causes and effects or between the prelude to and the results of the circumstances and events that preceded 2 August, and what took place on 2 August and afterward, have been missed.

This description was in most cases applicable to some Arabs and to many foreigners, so that some of them could not remember what Zionism and US imperialism have done against Iraq, beginning with the Irangate plot or the Iran-contra scandal in 1986 until the first months of 1990, when the plot against Iraq reached its dangerous phases, as US and Western media began to prepare for the Israeli aggression against us, which we confronted in the statement of 8 April 1990: when the Americans cut off bread from Iraq and canceled the grain deal concluded with US companies in the third month of the same year, that is 1990; and when they raised the slogan of an economic, technologic, and scientific boycott of Iraq and worked to make Europe and Japan do the same.

We know that recalling the preludes and causes leading up to the results and recalling the grounds for an event or events in a permanent manner and in all (?cases) is not an easy undertaking. This is because doing so requires a high degree of awareness, or because this requires a vital connection between those recalling the backgrounds and preludes to these events, and the kind of immediate and long-term suffering produced by their causes and effects.

Those whom we describe as forgetful or as unaware of the connection between a given cause and a given effect do not all enjoy the same degree of awareness that provides the elements of (word indistinct) what is required. Most of them have not suffered the causes and effects of the circumstances, especially in the world arena. Therefore, we have faced serious difficulties in making them understand that what happened on 2 August, despite the clarity of the entirely just historic dimension, is basically not a cause within the course of the conflict between Iraq — as a bastion of faith and honorable aspiration — and Zionism and US imperialism. The events of that day are one aspect of the results of the battle or the conflict that preceded 2 August. The measure taken on the glorious day of the call is a means of self-defense, and one aimed at defending all honorable principles and values of Iraq. Although (words indistinct) an offensive form, an account of the events of this day should not be taken out from the general context of developments. A correct account of this requires that it be placed within its comprehensive framework.

The failure of some world circles, especially among politicians who are (?outspoken) against the Arabs (word indistinct), to understand has been boosted by the fact that, regardless of the details, the objective of these circles is to harm Iraq's accomplishments.

Some tyrannical Arab rulers, who betrayed the nation's principles and aspirations of their peoples, cooperated with and stooped to this tendency. They accepted degradation and humiliation, even inside the palaces and seats of their rule. They chose the path of obeying the tendentious foreigner and his evil, hostile intentions.

This flood of media campaigns officially conducted against us by 30 countries further complicated the prospect of establishing a link between causes and effects and between what happened to the Arabs and to the Iraqis prior to 2 August, what happened on the day of the call to glory, and what happened after 2 August. All the accumulated extensions and influences of these countries accompany these campaigns, and are affected by them. Nevertheless, the noble person has remained noble and is guided by the facts — not merely by what he sees and hears, but along the path where his heart, his faithful empathy with jihad, and his destiny with the Iraqi stance lead him. This is the stance of the people in this nation. What has guided them in this direction has been their long suffering at the hands of the ranks of injustice, the unjust, and the Arab rulers who are their allies and who betrayed the nation and sold out honor and religion to the foreigner. Some of those rulers chose this course as an indispensable path to assuming their places on the seat of power and undeservedly impose themselves on their people. It was the down payment for their agentry. Other rulers stooped to this after they discovered, taking into account the nature of rule they have chosen, that there was no other way to keep the seat of power except to comply with the will of the US intelligence services. This applies without exception to the Arab rulers who are siding with the United States today and supplying its aggression under the Arab cover and with funds it needs, and with the false and fraudulent talk of Arab ability. Evil is what they are doing.

Traitor Fahd, the betrayer of the two mosques, and light-headed Husni, the ruler with which noble Arab Egypt has been afflicted, stand at the head of the list. Faced with this state of affairs, we found that the enemy media and the enemy policy dropped a heavy screen on every event, stand, or cause that preceded 2 August 1990 that could shed some light on these incidents and explain their true nature. Palestine, whose just cause dates back more than 40 years, as well as its future and the positions on it, has been one of the most important pillars of the conspiracy in which the oil rulers have participated as conspirators against Iraq, led by the agent shaykhs of Kuwait and the Saudi rulers. Biased people have even tried to neglect the fate of Palestine as being one of the causes of these events. The tendentious media, which have widespread influence and impact, and the suspect politicians and those who seek personal objectives — backed by Zionism everywhere — began to focus on the 2 August events to depict them as having taken place without any basis or background and as though our attention were being devoted only to these events. They even issued orders to silence voices and prevent them from mentioning any historical background that would explain to the foreigner or the Arab what he does not know about the reality of the relationship that exists between Kuwait and Iraq, and that Kuwait is part of Iraq, but was severed following the partitioning conspiracy used to weaken the Arab nation, harm its status and role, and weaken every Arab country that has some kind of leverage.

In view of this deluge of the falsification of facts, and because of this large number of countries participating in the aggression — or those who have been confused about the real reasons for the results — it is insufficient to respond and clarify through media and political statements alone, in view of our modest influence. Measures and actions are inevitable to place the innocent, who do not know the (?aspect of links), before a rational debate that bypasses the smokescreens and misinformation launched by hostile information media. Something must be done to place the enemies in an embarrassing situation or in an impasse — something that will drive them to behavior and positions that will make those who have been anesthetized by hostile media wake up to new facts or new (?opportunities) that will reveal to them the facts, free from covers, so that they can appear as they are, crystal clear. Thus came the 15 February initiative (another version of the 12 August "linkage" plan), which the Revolution Command Council statement fired at the enemy goal — to use the terms of sports and athletics — so as to shake the nets of the enemy court. Either an acceptance that pleases friends or rejection that annoys the enemies (sentence as heard). This may divide the enemy ranks, which are founded on rancor and rallied around wrong. Certain people who have been misled will discover what will help them realize that what has happened, and the root of what has happened, was not caused by 2 August and what followed. What preceded 2 August does not go back to 1990, its events, and circumstances alone, but goes back to every iota of dignity and pride, faith and tenacity toward right, rejection of wrong, and hostility to criminal usurper Zionism, support for the poor, and the fight against injustice and corruption. These stands are the qualities of Iraqis, or what has been revived in them by the revolutionary leadership.

The rancor against Iraq has been created over time, with every aspect of capability added to Iraq or created to become a serious pillar of its characteristics and potential; with steadfastness in the face of the aggression exposing the weakness of some of the Arabs *vis-à-vis* the aggression of Zionism and the ambitions of the Americans; with every book that has been written with sweat in support of the blood of struggle; with every effort and every stage of building in Iraq's lofty edifice; with every floor in the building of its new civilization or wheel in every factory or plant which has been built as a symbol of loftiness and as an introduction to a new, happy, and prosperous life under firm faith in God, the homeland, and the nation; and with the slogan: The poor have a right in the wealth of the rich, because they are members of the same people or members of the same nation, and all of them are the sons of Adam and Eve.

To those who ask about the rancor of Husni and others like him toward the leadership and people of Iraq, and to those who were alarmed by this rancor harbored by those who ate and drank under Iraqi hospitality and were given attention which they do not deserve, we say that we do not regret the hospitality and good intentions accorded by us or the people of Iraq toward people whom we wanted, at the time, to be brothers of the Iraqis, when they stood in the ranks of the faithful, with noble convictions and honorable intentions. But since they have committed treason, no one will feel sorry for them. May God's curse be upon them until the day of judgment. We say that these misled people have derived their rancor against you, O Iraqis, and against your leadership, from the attributes which you possess and which have characterized your leadership. These misled people have apparently found in every call for honor and purity of intention and in every call stating that the ruler or leader should be part of his people, an insult aimed against [them] personally by the people of Iraq and its leadership.

Each placard you raised when you went out to receive them, those who rejected the Zionist scheme and US imperialism and denounced their agents, was viewed by them as a placard directed against them. Each word said about the importance of the fairness of the ruler or leader and about his lightweight guilt when the money he carries is lightweight, was considered a personal attack against them. Each denunciation of weakness, submissiveness, and the acceptance of humiliation was an insult to them.

Yes, noble mujahidin sons of Iraq, that group of Arabs, and maybe other rulers, and even some foreigners, have found that every positive feature in you and your structure reflects in a shining mirror their shortcomings and defects before the people and the nation. Each call for power, invincibility, faith, capability, nobility, pride, dignity, courage, liberation from the foreigner, abstinence, and the liberation of the soul from ill-gotten money; and each attempt to highlight the correct qualities of an official, in accordance with Arab and Muslim standards, was considered an instigation against them and a call to and indoctrination of their peoples to triumph over them.

It seems this is why some Arab rulers were filled with hatred against you. This, along with covetous designs, is also the reason that may fill some foreigners with hatred against you. But, brothers and sons, stalwart and honest men and glorious women, what more can we do? Would anything other than this have left even a grain of honor, faith, glory, and pride; or would it have left a gift that we would take pride in and a future toward whose doors and shining promises we race?

Would any action to the contrary — in which we would follow the heels of the foreigner in the direction that he wants — leave a drop of honor for the men and free women? Would any such act leave faith and its rites anything but decaying bones and fine dust that meet no need? Is there (?anything) that our great Iraqi people and glorious nation takes pride in other than this course? We will all maintain our character and will demand anything else that will boost and entrench faith and cleanse souls to the satisfaction of (word indistinct) and nation.

There is no other course than the one we have chosen, except the course of humiliation and darkness, after which there will be no bright sign in the sky or brilliant light on earth. We have chosen this course. The Iraqis have chosen this course in an era where many characteristics become manifest. They continue to ask and work for what will make them more brilliant, faithful, and lofty. There is no other course. We will protect it with our souls, funds, and hearts. We will proceed on this course, irrespective of the nature of the political efforts which we are exerting and whose formulation and directions Tariq 'Aziz carried to Moscow, and which, if rejected, will expose all the covers, and will only maintain the premeditated intentions of the aggression against us without any cover and without any slogans that will lead to *al-tadakhul* (intermingling). After the 15 February initiative sprang from its sister initiative of 12 August 1990, what did Bush say, and what did his servant Fahd say? Bush rejected it and regarded it as a cruel hoax before he understood it. Fahd, who chews his words just as camels chew the grass of their pastures, became an eloquent orator to say the war against Iraq will continue until Iraq does this and that. Note, O observers, note, O people who have been distracted by the 2 August events from the real intentions of the aggression, note and examine that which you have overlooked. The Iraqis and good people became aware of it at an early date. Note how Bush and Fahd have designs regarding matters that were not included among their slogans, either before or after 2 August, and not until a short time ago. Note how they now have ambitions for greater things — light-headed Husni speaks in the same strain — to reveal their true intentions and not accept the 15 February initiative. Remember how in the period that preceded the announcement of the initiative, they and others in the West said that as soon as the word withdrawal is said, everything will be possible afterward. Note how they now have revealed their greed more clearly than they did, even in the moment preceding the announcement of the initiative. Note what their media are talking about now. These media are speaking about depriving Iraq of strength and capability and of the manifestations of progress, honor, and good examples. They want to deprive Iraq of every quality characterizing truly faithful people and good sons who are faithful to their people, homeland, and nation. Shame on them, and shame on their cowardly act, and shame on all they do.

Note how those who, at one stage of the struggle, wanted to make the word withdrawal an introduction to undermining our armed forces' determination and resolve, and wanted to sow disarray in the ranks of our armed forces, are no longer interested in such a word now, or so they claim. They have started to neglect it and to talk about what is new, now that this has become a gratuitous gain, as they believe. They forgot that our people and armed forces — in addition to their evident great determination for jihad, which is a dowry to the wedding of jihad and sacrifice — are also fully aware that every step we make should be countered by what it deserves in terms of guarantees and by an action that keeps the future open before the Iraqis and the Arabs and all the faithful who reject injustice in the world, and that the word withdrawal has been placed by the Iraqis, the Arabs, and the good men of this world within this context and within the proper framework.

From this premise, and in the context of the comprehensive approach, it is the entire 15 February initiative, as a new beginning, that will make the Iraqis more determined and more resolved if the initiative is rejected. Our armed forces will become more capable. This will result from the exposure of pretexts and disclosure of the true nature of the premeditated intentions. All this will make them more patient and steadfast and better prepared for the battle which God blesses and which good men support, after which there will be only a glorious conclusion, where a brilliant sun will clear the dust of battle, and where the clouds of battles will be dispelled to make room for a brilliant moon surrounded by a halo, whose size will be commensurate with the sacrifices that are required by the duties and conditions of victory, and by the patience that God almighty expects from the people of jihad.

O brothers, O people, note how those who feared a ground battle have now avoided the showdown for over a month. They have persisted further in killing civilians (word indistinct) and destroying property with their long-range aircraft and missiles with rancor that dwarfs that of Hulagu (grandson of Mongol ruler Genghis Khan). They are doing this in an (?expression) to cover up their inability to confront our land forces in southern Iraq. Note how they, and certain people who do not know the Iraqis' faith and capability, now portray matters in a way as though the mere fact of not launching the land offensive is a gain to Iraq that the Iraqis should respond to with further concessions that would harm their principles, dignity, and rights as well as the Arab nation's rights and security. Notice how they are indulging in illusions. With any initiative, Iraq seeks to establish peace in the Gulf that will open the door to a comprehensive and equitable solution that achieves a real and permanent peace in the region in its entirety—foremost in Palestine. Iraq does not seek a temporary truce or capitulation which the failure and shameful want or have illusions about the possibility of achieving.

O fair people, note all this, as the Iraqis have noted, acknowledged, and concluded. Note all this so as to excuse the Iraqis from any subsequent action and to understand the justness of the Iraqi position. God is great, and mercy and immortality for our martyrs and our nation. Dignity, glory, and victory for the heroes of this path, the sons of our nation and mankind. God is great, God is great. Accursed be the lowly.

Source: FBIS-NES-91-035, 21 February 1991.

21. Saddam Husayn Speaks on Allies' Ground Attack
24 February 1991

Speech by President Saddam Husayn, place not given — unclear whether live or recorded. *Baghdad Domestic Service in Arabic 0737 GMT, 24 February 1991.*

In the name of God, the compassionate, the merciful. It is possible that ye dislike a thing which is good for you and that ye love a thing which is bad for you. And God knoweth and ye know not (Koranic verses). O great Iraqi people, O valiant men of our heroic armed forces. O faithful and honorable people wherever you are among the sons of our nation and humanity.

At the time it was decided that the UN Security Council would meet to look into the Soviet peace initiative, which we endorsed, the treacherous committed treachery. The despicable Bush and his filthy agent Fahd and others who have consorted with them in committing crimes, shame, and aggression, committed the treachery. Those cowards who have perfected the acts of treachery, treason, and vileness committed treachery after they departed from every path of virtue, goodness, and humanity. They have committed treachery and waged their large-scale ground assault on our struggling forces this morning. Their objective became known to all who have not known their objective so far. They committed treachery according to their wont and qualities. They even betrayed those who along with them signed the infamous resolutions which were adopted at the UN Security Council prior to the military aggression against our country. They deluded themselves by believing that with those resolutions they were protecting international legitimacy. They betrayed everyone. God, however, is above everyone. He is the one and only, the living and almighty, the eternal and omnipotent. He will [rebound] their treachery on their necks and shame them until their ranks and their failing hordes are repulsed.

From the beginning, the evil ones worked on this path, the path of hostility and evil, to harm the Iraqi people and smother the shining candle in their hearts. Cursed be their intentions and cursed be their deeds. However, they will realize after a while that God's unshakable desire will prevent them from inflicting evil on the people of faith and jihad. They will realize after a while that the great people of Iraq and the brave Iraqi armed forces are not like what they think or imagine.

Fight them, O Iraqis, with all the values that you inherited from your great history and with all the values of faith in which you believed as a people who believe in God and who are proud of their dignity and their right to make choices and decisions.

Fight them, O brave, splendid men, O men of the Mother of Battles and al-Qadisiyya. Fight them with your faith in God. Fight them in defense of every free and honorable woman and every innocent child and in defense of the values of manhood, values, and the military honor which you shoulder. Fight them because with their defeat you will be at the last entrance of the victory of victories. The war will end with all that the situation entails of dignity, glory, and triumph for your people, army, and nation. If the opposite takes place, God forbid, there will only be the ignominious abyss to which the enemies are aspiring to push you so that Iraq, the (Arab) nation, and humanity might live in the darkness of a long night. Fight them, O men. They do not carry the values that entitle them to be more manly, courageous, and capable than you.

As men collide with each other, the weapons of supremacy will disappear and the only thing that remains to decide the final result will be the faith of the faithful and the courage of those who adhere to their noble, nationalistic, and faithful stand of jihad.

Fight them and show no mercy toward them, for this is how God wishes the faithful to fight the infidel. Your sons, mothers, fathers, and kin, and the entire population of Iraq and the world are beholding your performance today. Do what pleases God and brings dignity to the homeland and the people. Fight them in the style of faithful men. They are the camp of atheism, hypocrisy, and treachery, and you are the camp of faith, unshifting principles, loyalty, and sincerity.

Fight them and victory will be yours, as will be dignity, honor and glory. God is great. God is great. God is great. Let the miserable meet their fate. Victory is sweet with the help of God.

Source: FBIS-NES-91-037, 25 February 1991.

22. Saddam Husayn Speaks on Withdrawal From Kuwait
26 February 1991

Speech by President Saddam Husayn on 26 February 1991, place not given — unclear whether live or recorded. *Baghdad Domestic Service in Arabic 0824 GMT, 26 February 1991.*

In the name of God, the merciful, the compassionate. O great people, O stalwart men in the forces of jihad and faith, glorious men of the Mother of Battles, O zealous, faithful, and sincere people in our glorious nations, and among all Muslims and all virtuous people in the world, O glorious Iraqi women, in such circumstances and times, it is difficult to talk about all that should be talked about, and it is difficult to recall all that has to be recalled. Despite this, we have to recall what has to be recalled, and say part — a principal part — of what should be said.

We start by saying that on this day, our valiant armed forces will complete their withdrawal from Kuwait. And on this day, our fight against aggression and the ranks of infidelity, joined in an ugly coalition comprising 30 countries, which officially entered war against us under the leadership of the United States of America — our fight against them would have lasted from the first month of this year, starting with the night of 16–17 January, until this moment in the current month, February. It was an epic duel which lasted for two months, which came to confirm clearly a lesson that God has wanted as a prelude of faith, impregnability, and capability for the faithful, and a prelude to an (?abyss), weakness, and humiliation which God almighty has wanted for the infidels, the criminals, the traitors, the corrupt and the deviators.

To be added to this is the military and nonmilitary duel, including the military and the economic blockade, which was imposed on Iraq and which lasted throughout 1990 until today, and until the time God almighty wishes it to last.

Before that, the duel lasted in other forms for years before this time. It was an epic struggle between right and wrong; we have talked about this in detail on previous occasions.

It gave depth to the age of the showdown for the year 1990, and the already elapsed part of the year 1991. Hence, we do not forget, because we will not forget this great struggling spirit, by which men of great faith stormed the fortifications and the weapons of deception and the Croesus' (Kuwaiti rulers) treachery on the honorable day of the call. They did what they did within the context of legitimate deterrence and great principled action.

All that we have gone through or decided within its circumstances, obeying God's will and choosing a position of faith and chivalry is a record of honor, the significance of which will not be missed by the people and nation and the values of Islam and humanity. Their days will continue to be glorious, and their past and future will continue to relate the story of a faithful, jealous, and patient people who believed in the will of God and in the values and stands accepted by the almighty for the Arab nation in its leading role and for the Islamic nation in the essentials of its true faith and how they should be. These values — which had their effect in all those situations, offered the sacrifices they had offered in the struggle, and symbolized the depth of the faithful character in Iraq — will continue to leave their effects on souls. They will continue to reap their harvest, not only in terms of direct targets represented in the slogans of their age — whether in the conflict between the oppressed poor and the unjust and opportunist rich, or between faith and blasphemy, or between injustice, deception, and treachery on the one hand and fairness, justice, honesty, and loyalty on the other — but also the indirect targets as well. This will shake the opposite ranks and cause them to collapse after everything has become clear. This will also add faith to the faithful, now that the minds and eyes have been opened and the hearts are longing for what the principles, values, and stances should long for and belong to.

The stage that preceded the great day of the call on 2 August 1990 had its own standards, including dealing with what is familiar and inherited during the bad times, whether on the level of relations between the ruler and the ruled, or between the leader and the people he leads. The relations between the foreigners among the ranks of infidelity and oppression and among the region's states and the world had their own standards, effects, and privileges that were created by the Arab homeland's circumstances, and which were facilitated by propaganda, which no one could expose more than it has now been exposed. The conflict was exacerbated by the vacuum that was created by the weakness of one of the two poles that used to represent the two opposite lines in the world. After 2 August 1990, however, new concepts and standards were created. This was preceded by a new outlook in all walks of life, in relations among peoples, relations among states, the relations between the ruler and the ruled, and by standards of faith and positions; patriotism, pan-Arabism, and humanitarianism; jihad, faith, Islam, fear and non-fear; restlessness and tranquility; manhood and its opposite; struggle, jihad, and sacrifice; and readiness to do good things and their opposite.

When new measures spring forth and the familiar, failed, traitorous, subservient, corrupt (people) and tyrants are rejected, then the opportunity for the cultivation of the pure soil will increase in its scope, and the seeds of this plant will take root deep in the good land, primarily the land of the Arabs, and the land of revelation and the messages, and the land of prophets. God says: "Like a goodly tree, whose root is firmly fixed, and its branches reach to the heavens. It brings forth its fruit at all times, by the leave of its Lord" (Koranic verse).

Then, everything will become possible on the road of goodness and happiness that is not defiled by the feet of the invaders nor by their evil will or the corruption of the corrupt among those who have been corrupted, and who spread corruption in the land of the Arabs. Moreover, the forces of plotting and treachery will be defeated for good. Good people and those who are distinguished by their faith and by their faithful, honorable stands of jihad will become the real leaders of the gathering of the faithful everywhere on earth, and the gathering of the corruption, falsehood, hypocrisy, and infidelity will be defeated and meet the vilest fate. The earth will be inherited, at God's order, by His righteous slaves. "For the earth is God's to give as a heritage to such of His servants as He pleaseth; and the end is best for the righteous" (Koranic verse).

When this happens, the near objectives will not only be within reach, available and possible, but also the doors will be open without any hindrance which might prevent the achievement of all the greater, remoter, and more comprehensive objectives to the Arabs, Muslims, and humanity at large.

Then, also, it will be clear that the harvest does not precede the seeding, and that the threshing floor and the yield are the outcome of a successful seeding and a successful harvest.

The harvest in the Mother of Battles has succeeded. After we have harvested what we have harvested, the greater harvest and its yield will be in the time to come, and it will be much greater than what we have at present, in spite of what we have at present in terms of the victory, dignity, and glory that was based on the sacrifices of a deep faith which is generous without any hesitation or fear. It is by virtue of this faith that God has bestowed dignity upon the Iraqi mujahidin and upon all the depth of this course of jihad at the level of the Arab homeland and at the level of all those men whom God has chosen to be given the honor of allegiance, guidance, and honorable position, until He declares that the conflict has stopped, or amends its directions and course and the positions in a manner which would please the faithful and increase their dignity.

O valiant Iraqi men, O glorious Iraqi women, Kuwait is part of your country and was carved from it in the past. Circumstances today have willed that it remain in the state in which it will remain after the withdrawal of our struggling forces from it. It hurts you that this should happen.

We rejoiced on the day of the call when it was decided that Kuwait should be one of the main gates for deterring the plot and for defending all Iraq from the plotters. We say that we will remember Kuwait on the great day of the call, on the days that followed it, and in documents and events, some of which date back 70 years.

The Iraqis will remember and will not forget that on 8 August 1990 Kuwait became part of Iraq legally, constitutionally, and actually. They remember and will not forget that it remained throughout this period from 8 August 1990 until last night, when withdrawal began, and today we will complete withdrawal of our forces, God willing. Today, certain circumstances made the Iraqi Army withdraw as a result of the ramifications which we mentioned, including the combined aggression by 30 countries. Their repugnant siege had been led in evil and aggression by the machine and the criminal entity of America and its major allies.

These malicious ranks took the depth and effectiveness of their aggressiveness not only from the aggressive premeditated intentions against Iraq, the Arab nation, and Islam, but also from the position of those who were deceived by the claim of international legitimacy. Everyone will remember that the gates of Constantinople were not opened before the Muslims in the first struggling attempt, and that the international community (?consigned) dear Palestine's freedom and independence to oblivion.

Whatever the suspect parties try, by virtue of the sacrifices and struggle of the Palestinians and Iraqis, Palestine has returned anew to knock at the doors closed on evil.

Palestine returned to knock on those doors to force the tyrants and the traitors to a solution that would place it at the forefront of the issues that have to be resolved — a solution that would bring dignity to its people and provide better chances for better progress.

The issue of poverty and richness, fairness and unfairness, faith and infidelity, treachery and honesty and sincerity, have become titles corresponding to rare events and well-known people and trends that give priority to what is positive over what is negative, to what is sincere over what is treacherous and filthy, and to what is pure and honorable over what is corrupt, base, and lowly. The confidence of the nationalists and the faithful mujahidin and the Muslims has grown bigger than before, and hope grew more and more. Slogans have come out of their stores to occupy strongly the facades of the pan-Arab and human jihad and struggle. Therefore, victory is (?great), now and in the future, God willing.

Shout for victory, O brothers, shout for your victory and the victory of all honorable people, O Iraqis. You have fought 30 countries, and all the evil and the largest machine of war and destruction in the world that surrounds them. If only one of these countries threatens anyone, this threat will have a swift and direct effect on the dignity, freedom, or life of this or that country, people, and nation.

The soldiers of faith have triumphed over the soldiers of wrong. O stalwart men, your God is the one who granted your victory. You triumphed when you rejected, in the name of faith, the will of evil which the evildoers wanted to impose on you to kill the fire of faith in your hearts. You have chosen the path you have chosen, including acceptance of the Soviet initiative, but those evildoers persisted in their path and methods, thinking that they can impose their will on Iraq, as they imagined and hoped. This hope of theirs may remain in their heads, even after we withdraw from Kuwait. Therefore, we must be cautious, and preparedness to fight must remain at the highest level.

O you valiant men, you have fought the armies of 30 states and the capabilities of an even greater number of states which supplied them with the means of aggression and support. Faith, belief, hope, and determination continue to fill your chests, souls, and hearts. They have even become deeper, stronger, brighter, and more deeply rooted. God is great, God is great, may the lowly be defeated. Victory is sweet with the help of God.

Source: FBIS-NES-90-038, 26 February 1991.